On
Building a Great Culture

HBR's 10 Must Reads series is the definitive collection of ideas and best practices for aspiring and experienced leaders alike. These books offer essential reading selected from the pages of *Harvard Business Review* on topics critical to the success of every manager.

Titles include:

HBR's 10 Must Reads 2015
HBR's 10 Must Reads 2016
HBR's 10 Must Reads 2017
HBR's 10 Must Reads 2018
HBR's 10 Must Reads 2019
HBR's 10 Must Reads 2020
HBR's 10 Must Reads for CEOs
HBR's 10 Must Reads for New Managers
HBR's 10 Must Reads on AI, Analytics, and the New Machine Age
HBR's 10 Must Reads on Business Model Innovation
HBR's 10 Must Reads on Change Management
HBR's 10 Must Reads on Collaboration
HBR's 10 Must Reads on Communication
HBR's 10 Must Reads on Diversity
HBR's 10 Must Reads on Emotional Intelligence
HBR's 10 Must Reads on Entrepreneurship and Startups
HBR's 10 Must Reads on Innovation
HBR's 10 Must Reads on Leadership
HBR's 10 Must Reads on Leadership for Healthcare
HBR's 10 Must Reads on Leadership Lessons from Sports
HBR's 10 Must Reads on Making Smart Decisions
HBR's 10 Must Reads on Managing Across Cultures
HBR's 10 Must Reads on Managing People
HBR's 10 Must Reads on Managing Yourself
HBR's 10 Must Reads on Mental Toughness
HBR's 10 Must Reads on Negotiation
HBR's 10 Must Reads on Nonprofits and the Social Sectors

HBR's 10 Must Reads on Reinventing HR
HBR's 10 Must Reads on Sales
HBR's 10 Must Reads on Strategic Marketing
HBR's 10 Must Reads on Strategy
HBR's 10 Must Reads on Strategy for Healthcare
HBR's 10 Must Reads on Teams
HBR's 10 Must Reads on Women and Leadership
HBR's 10 Must Reads: The Essentials

HBR'S 10 MUST READS

On
Building
a Great
Culture

HARVARD BUSINESS REVIEW PRESS
Boston, Massachusetts

Library of Congress Cataloging-in-Publication Data

Title: HBR's 10 must reads on building a great culture / Harvard Business Review.
Other titles: HBR's ten must reads on building a great culture | HBR's 10 must reads (Series)
Description: Boston, Massachusetts : Harvard Business Review Press, [2020] | Series: HBR's 10 must reads | Includes index.
Identifiers: LCCN 2019030904 | ISBN 9781633698062 (paperback)
Subjects: LCSH: Corporate culture. | Leadership.
Classification: LCC HD58.7 .H42 2019 | DDC 658—dc 23
LC record available at https://lccn.loc.gov/2019030904

ISBN: 978-1-63369-806-2
eISBN: 978-1-63369-807-9

The paper used in this publication meets the requirements of the American National Standard for Permanence of Paper for Publications and Documents in Libraries and Archives Z39.48-1992.

Contents

On
Building
a Great
Culture

The Leader's Guide to Corporate Culture

by Boris Groysberg, Jeremiah Lee, Jesse Price, and J. Yo-Jud Cheng

STRATEGY AND CULTURE ARE AMONG the primary levers at top leaders' disposal in their never-ending quest to maintain organizational viability and effectiveness. Strategy offers a formal logic for the company's goals and orients people around them. Culture expresses goals through values and beliefs and guides activity through shared assumptions and group norms.

Strategy provides clarity and focus for collective action and decision making. It relies on plans and sets of choices to mobilize people and can often be enforced by both concrete rewards for achieving goals and consequences for failing to do so. Ideally, it also incorporates adaptive elements that can scan and analyze the external environment and sense when changes are required to maintain continuity and growth. Leadership goes hand-in-hand with strategy formation, and most leaders understand the fundamentals. Culture, however, is a more elusive lever, because much of it is anchored in unspoken behaviors, mindsets, and social patterns.

For better *and* worse, culture and leadership are inextricably linked. Founders and influential leaders often set new cultures in motion and imprint values and assumptions that persist for decades. Over time an organization's leaders can also shape culture, through both conscious and unconscious actions (sometimes with unintended consequences).

1

The best leaders we have observed are fully aware of the multiple cultures within which they are embedded, can sense when change is required, and can deftly influence the process.

Unfortunately, in our experience it is far more common for leaders seeking to build high-performing organizations to be confounded by culture. Indeed, many either let it go unmanaged or relegate it to the HR function, where it becomes a secondary concern for the business. They may lay out detailed, thoughtful plans for strategy and execution, but because they don't understand culture's power and dynamics, their plans go off the rails. As someone once said, culture eats strategy for breakfast.

It doesn't have to be that way. Our work suggests that culture can, in fact, be managed. The first and most important step leaders can take to maximize its value and minimize its risks is to become fully aware of how it works. By integrating findings from more than 100 of the most commonly used social and behavioral models, we have identified eight styles that distinguish a culture and can be measured. (We gratefully acknowledge the rich history of cultural studies—going all the way back to the earliest explorations of human nature—on which our work builds.) Using this framework, leaders can model the impact of culture on their business and assess its alignment with strategy. We also suggest how culture can help them achieve change and build organizations that thrive in even the most trying times.

Defining Culture

Culture is the tacit social order of an organization: It shapes attitudes and behaviors in wide-ranging and durable ways. Cultural norms define what is encouraged, discouraged, accepted, or rejected within a group. When properly aligned with personal values, drives, and needs, culture can unleash tremendous amounts of energy toward a shared purpose and foster an organization's capacity to thrive.

Culture can also evolve flexibly and autonomously in response to changing opportunities and demands. Whereas strategy is typically determined by the C-suite, culture can fluidly blend the

Idea in Brief

Executives are often confounded by culture, because much of it is anchored in unspoken behaviors, mindsets, and social patterns. Many leaders either let it go unmanaged or relegate it to HR, where it becomes a secondary concern for the business. This is a mistake, because properly managed, culture can help them achieve change and build organizations that will thrive in even the most trying times.

The authors have reviewed the literature on culture and distilled eight distinct culture styles: *caring*, focused on relationships and mutual trust; *purpose*, exemplified by idealism and altruism; *learning*, characterized by exploration, expansiveness, and creativity; *enjoyment*, expressed through fun and excitement; *results*, characterized by achievement and winning; *authority*, defined by strength, decisiveness, and boldness; *safety*, defined by planning, caution, and preparedness; and *order*, focused on respect, structure, and shared norms.

These eight styles fit into an "integrated culture framework"

according to the degree to which they reflect independence or interdependence (people interactions) and flexibility or stability (response to change). They can be used to diagnose and describe highly complex and diverse behavioral patterns in a culture and to model how likely an individual leader is to align with and shape that culture.

Through research and practical experience, the authors have arrived at five insights regarding culture's effect on companies' success: (1) When aligned with strategy and leadership, a strong culture drives positive organizational outcomes. (2) Selecting or developing leaders for the future requires a forward-looking strategy and culture. (3) In a merger, designing a new culture on the basis of complementary strengths can speed up integration and create more value over time. (4) In a dynamic, uncertain environment, in which organizations must be more agile, learning gains importance. (5) A strong culture can be a significant liability when it is misaligned with strategy.

intentions of top leaders with the knowledge and experiences of frontline employees.

The academic literature on the subject is vast. Our review of it revealed many formal definitions of organizational culture and a variety of models and methods for assessing it. Numerous processes exist for creating and changing it. Agreement on specifics is sparse across these definitions, models, and methods, but through a synthesis of seminal work by Edgar Schein, Shalom Schwartz, Geert Hofstede, and other leading scholars, we have identified four generally accepted attributes:

Shared

Culture is a group phenomenon. It cannot exist solely within a single person, nor is it simply the average of individual characteristics. It resides in shared behaviors, values, and assumptions and is most commonly experienced through the norms and expectations of a group—that is, the unwritten rules.

Pervasive

Culture permeates multiple levels and applies very broadly in an organization; sometimes it is even conflated with the organization itself. It is manifest in collective behaviors, physical environments, group rituals, visible symbols, stories, and legends. Other aspects of culture are unseen, such as mindsets, motivations, unspoken assumptions, and what David Rooke and William Torbert refer to as "action logics" (mental models of how to interpret and respond to the world around you).

Enduring

Culture can direct the thoughts and actions of group members over the long term. It develops through critical events in the collective life and learning of a group. Its endurance is explained in part by the attraction-selection-attrition model first introduced by Benjamin Schneider: People are drawn to organizations with characteristics similar to their own; organizations are more likely to select individuals who seem to "fit in"; and over time those who don't fit in tend to leave. Thus culture becomes a self-reinforcing social pattern that grows increasingly resistant to change and outside influences.

Implicit

An important and often overlooked aspect of culture is that despite its subliminal nature, people are effectively hardwired to recognize and respond to it instinctively. It acts as a kind of silent language.

Shalom Schwartz and E.O. Wilson have shown through their research how evolutionary processes shaped human capacity; because the ability to sense and respond to culture is universal, certain themes should be expected to recur across the many models, definitions, and studies in the field. That is exactly what we have discovered in our research over the past few decades.

Eight Distinct Culture Styles

Our review of the literature for commonalities and central concepts revealed two primary dimensions that apply regardless of organization type, size, industry, or geography: people interactions and response to change. Understanding a company's culture requires determining where it falls along these two dimensions.

People interactions

An organization's orientation toward people interactions and coordination will fall on a spectrum from highly independent to highly interdependent. Cultures that lean toward the former place greater value on autonomy, individual action, and competition. Those that lean toward the latter emphasize integration, managing relationships, and coordinating group effort. People in such cultures tend to collaborate and to see success through the lens of the group.

Response to change

Whereas some cultures emphasize stability—prioritizing consistency, predictability, and maintenance of the status quo—others emphasize flexibility, adaptability, and receptiveness to change. Those that favor stability tend to follow rules, use control structures such as seniority-based staffing, reinforce hierarchy, and strive for efficiency. Those that favor flexibility tend to prioritize innovation, openness, diversity, and a longer-term orientation. (Kim Cameron, Robert Quinn, and Robert Ernest are among the researchers who employ similar dimensions in their culture frameworks.)

By applying this fundamental insight about the dimensions of people interactions and response to change, we have identified eight styles that apply to both organizational cultures and individual leaders. Researchers at Spencer Stuart (including two of this article's authors) have interdependently studied and refined this list of styles across both levels over the past two decades.

Caring focuses on relationships and mutual trust. Work environments are warm, collaborative, and welcoming places where people help and support one another. Employees are united by loyalty; leaders emphasize sincerity, teamwork, and positive relationships.

Purpose is exemplified by idealism and altruism. Work environments are tolerant, compassionate places where people try to do good for the long-term future of the world. Employees are united by a focus on sustainability and global communities; leaders emphasize shared ideals and contributing to a greater cause.

Learning is characterized by exploration, expansiveness, and creativity. Work environments are inventive and open-minded places where people spark new ideas and explore alternatives. Employees are united by curiosity; leaders emphasize innovation, knowledge, and adventure.

Enjoyment is expressed through fun and excitement. Work environments are lighthearted places where people tend to do what makes them happy. Employees are united by playfulness and stimulation; leaders emphasize spontaneity and a sense of humor.

Results is characterized by achievement and winning. Work environments are outcome-oriented and merit-based places where people aspire to achieve top performance. Employees are united by a drive for capability and success; leaders emphasize goal accomplishment.

Authority is defined by strength, decisiveness, and boldness. Work environments are competitive places where people strive to gain personal advantage. Employees are united by strong control; leaders emphasize confidence and dominance.

Safety is defined by planning, caution, and preparedness. Work environments are predictable places where people are risk-conscious and think things through carefully. Employees are united by a desire to feel protected and anticipate change; leaders emphasize being realistic and planning ahead.

Order is focused on respect, structure, and shared norms. Work environments are methodical places where people tend to play by the rules and want to fit in. Employees are united by cooperation; leaders emphasize shared procedures and time-honored customs.

These eight styles fit into our integrated culture framework (see the exhibit "Integrated culture: The framework") according to the degree to which they reflect independence or interdependence (people interactions) and flexibility or stability (response to change). Styles that are adjacent in the framework, such as *safety* and *order,* frequently coexist within organizations and their people. In contrast, styles that are located across from each other, such as *safety* and *learning,* are less likely to be found together and require more organizational energy to maintain simultaneously. Each style has advantages and disadvantages, and no style is inherently better than another. An organizational culture can be defined by the absolute and relative strengths of each of the eight and by the degree of employee agreement about which styles characterize the organization. A powerful feature of this framework, which differentiates it from other models, is that it can also be used to define individuals' styles and the values of leaders and employees.

Inherent in the framework are fundamental trade-offs. Although each style can be beneficial, natural constraints and competing demands force difficult choices about which values to emphasize and how people are expected to behave. It is common to find organizations with cultures that emphasize both *results* and *caring,* but this combination can be confusing to employees. Are they expected to optimize individual goals and strive for outcomes at all costs, or should they work as a team and emphasize collaboration and shared success? The nature of the work itself, the business strategy, or the design of the organization may make it difficult for employees to be equally *results* focused and *caring.*

In contrast, a culture that emphasizes *caring* and *order* encourages a work environment in which teamwork, trust, and respect are paramount. The two styles are mutually reinforcing, which can be beneficial but can also present challenges. The benefits are strong loyalty, retention of talent, lack of conflict, and high levels of engagement.

Integrated culture: The framework

On the basis of decades of experience analyzing organizations, executives, and employees, we developed a rigorous, comprehensive model to identify the key attributes of both group culture and individual leadership styles. Eight characteristics emerge when we map cultures along two dimensions: how people interact (independence to interdependence) and their response to change (flexibility to stability). The relative salience of these eight styles differs across organizations, though nearly all are strongly characterized by results *and* caring.

The spatial relationships are important. Proximate styles, such as safety *and* order, *or* learning *and* enjoyment, *will coexist more easily than styles that are far apart on the chart, such as* authority *and* purpose, *or* safety *and* learning. *Achieving a culture of* authority *often means gaining the advantages (and living with the disadvantages) of that culture but missing out on the advantages (and avoiding the disadvantages) of a culture of* purpose.

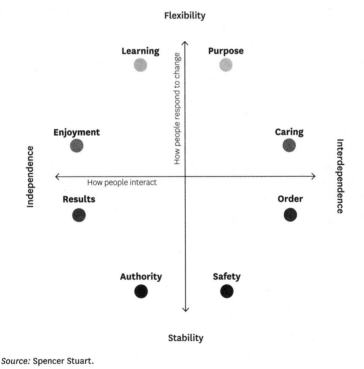

Source: Spencer Stuart.

Integrated culture: Leader statements

Top leaders and founders often express cultural sentiments within the public domain, either intentionally or unintentionally. Such statements can provide important clues to how these leaders are thinking about and leading their organizations' cultures.

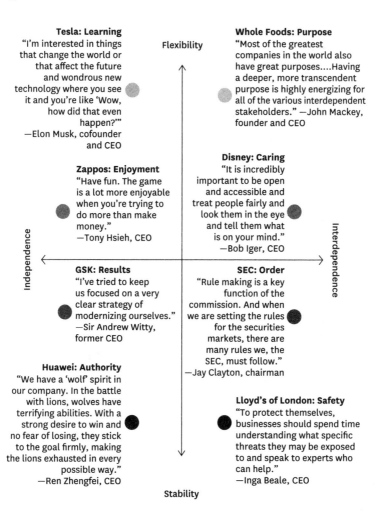

Tesla: Learning
"I'm interested in things that change the world or that affect the future and wondrous new technology where you see it and you're like 'Wow, how did that even happen?'"
—Elon Musk, cofounder and CEO

Flexibility

Whole Foods: Purpose
"Most of the greatest companies in the world also have great purposes....Having a deeper, more transcendent purpose is highly energizing for all of the various interdependent stakeholders." —John Mackey, founder and CEO

Zappos: Enjoyment
"Have fun. The game is a lot more enjoyable when you're trying to do more than make money."
—Tony Hsieh, CEO

Disney: Caring
"It is incredibly important to be open and accessible and treat people fairly and look them in the eye and tell them what is on your mind."
—Bob Iger, CEO

Independence

Interdependence

GSK: Results
"I've tried to keep us focused on a very clear strategy of modernizing ourselves."
—Sir Andrew Witty, former CEO

SEC: Order
"Rule making is a key function of the commission. And when we are setting the rules for the securities markets, there are many rules we, the SEC, must follow."
—Jay Clayton, chairman

Huawei: Authority
"We have a 'wolf' spirit in our company. In the battle with lions, wolves have terrifying abilities. With a strong desire to win and no fear of losing, they stick to the goal firmly, making the lions exhausted in every possible way."
—Ren Zhengfei, CEO

Lloyd's of London: Safety
"To protect themselves, businesses should spend time understanding what specific threats they may be exposed to and speak to experts who can help."
—Inga Beale, CEO

Stability

9

The pros and cons of culture styles

Every culture style has strengths and weaknesses. The table below summarizes the advantages and disadvantages of each style and how frequently it appears as a defining culture characteristic among the companies in our study.

Culture style	Advantages	Disadvantages	Ranked 1st or 2nd
Caring Warm, sincere, relational	Improved teamwork, engagement, communication, trust, and sense of belonging	Overemphasis on consensus building may reduce exploration of options, stifle competitiveness, and slow decision making	63%
Purpose Purpose-driven, idealistic, tolerant	Improved appreciation for diversity, sustainability, and social responsibility	Overemphasis on a long-term purpose and ideals may get in the way of practical and immediate concerns	9%
Learning Open, inventive, exploring	Improved innovation, agility, and organizational learning	Overemphasis on exploration may lead to a lack of focus and an inability to exploit existing advantages	7%
Enjoyment Playful, instinctive, fun-loving	Improved employee morale, engagement, and creativity	Overemphasis on autonomy and engagement may lead to a lack of discipline and create possible compliance or governance issues	2%

Results Achievement-driven, goal-focused	Improved execution, external focus, capability building, and goal achievement	Overemphasis on achieving results may lead to communication and collaboration breakdowns and higher levels of stress and anxiety	89%
Authority Bold, decisive, dominant	Improved speed of decision making and responsiveness to threats or crises	Overemphasis on strong authority and bold decision making may lead to politics, conflict, and a psychologically unsafe work environment	4%
Safety Realistic, careful, prepared	Improved risk management, stability, and business continuity	Overemphasis on standardization and formalization may lead to bureaucracy, inflexibility, and dehumanization of the work environment	8%
Order Rule-abiding, respectful, cooperative	Improved operational efficiency, reduced conflict, and greater civic-mindedness	Overemphasis on rules and traditions may reduce individualism, stifle creativity, and limit organizational agility	15%

Note: Sum of percentages is greater than 100 because styles were counted as dominant if they were ranked 1st or 2nd overall.

The challenges are a tendency toward groupthink, reliance on consensus-based decisions, avoidance of difficult issues, and a calcified sense of "us versus them." Leaders who are more focused on *results* and *learning* may find the combination of *caring* and *order* stifling when they seek to drive entrepreneurship and change. Savvy leaders make use of existing cultural strengths and have a nuanced understanding of how to initiate change. They might rely on the participative nature of a culture focused on *caring* and *order* to engage team members and simultaneously identify a *learning*-oriented "insider" who has the trust of his or her peers to advocate for change through relationship networks.

The eight styles can be used to diagnose and describe highly complex and diverse behavioral patterns in a culture and to model how likely an individual leader is to align with and shape that culture. Using this framework and multilevel approach, managers can:

- Understand their organization's culture and assess its intended and unintended effects

- Evaluate the level of consistency in employees' views of the culture

- Identify subcultures that may account for higher or lower group performance

- Pinpoint differences between legacy cultures during mergers and acquisitions

- Rapidly orient new executives to the culture they are joining and help them determine the most effective way to lead employees

- Measure the degree of alignment between individual leadership styles and organizational culture to determine what impact a leader might have

- Design an aspirational culture and communicate the changes necessary to achieve it

The Link Between Culture and Outcomes

Our research and practical experience have shown that when you are evaluating how culture affects outcomes, the context in which the organization operates—geographic region, industry, strategy, leadership, and company structure—matters, as does the strength of the culture. (See "Context, Conditions, and Culture," the sidebar at the end of this article.) What worked in the past may no longer work in the future, and what worked for one company may not work for another.

We have arrived at the following insights:

When aligned with strategy and leadership, a strong culture drives positive organizational outcomes

Consider the case of a best-in-class retailer headquartered in the United States. The company had viewed its first priority as providing top-notch customer service. It accomplished this with a simple rule—Do right by the customer—that encouraged employees to use their judgment when providing service. A core HR training practice was to help every salesperson see customer interactions as an opportunity to create "service stories that become legendary." Employees were reminded to define service from the customer's perspective, to constantly engage customers with questions geared toward understanding their specific needs and preferences, and to go beyond their expectations.

In measuring the culture of this company, we found that like many other large retailers, it was characterized primarily by a combination of *results* and *caring*. Unlike many other retailers, however, it had a culture that was also very flexible, *learning* oriented, and focused on *purpose*. As one top executive explained, "We have freedom as long as we take good care of the customer."

Furthermore, the company's values and norms were very clear to everyone and consistently shared throughout the organization. As the retailer expanded into new segments and geographies over the years, the leadership strove to maintain an intense customer focus without diluting its cherished culture. Although the company had historically focused on developing leaders from within—who were natural culture carriers—recruiting outsiders became necessary as it grew. The company preserved its culture through this change by carefully assessing new leaders and designing an onboarding process that reinforced core values and norms.

Culture is a powerful differentiator for this company because it is strongly aligned with strategy and leadership. Delivering outstanding customer service requires a culture and a mindset that emphasize achievement, impeccable service, and problem solving through autonomy and inventiveness. Not surprisingly, those qualities have led to a variety of positive outcomes for the company, including robust growth and international expansion, numerous customer service awards, and frequent appearances on lists of the best companies to work for.

Selecting or developing leaders for the future requires a forward-looking strategy and culture

The chief executive of an agriculture business was planning to retire, spurring rumors about a hostile takeover. The CEO was actively grooming a successor, an insider who had been with the company for more than 20 years. Our analysis revealed an organizational culture that strongly emphasized *caring* and *purpose*. As one leader reflected, "You feel like part of a large family when you become an employee at this company."

The potential successor understood the culture but was far more risk-averse (*safety*) and respectful of traditions (*order*) than the rest of the company. Given the takeover rumors, top leaders and managers told the CEO that they believed the company needed to take a more aggressive and action-oriented stance in the future. The board decided to consider the internal candidate alongside people from outside the company.

Three external candidates emerged: one who was aligned with the current culture (*purpose*), one who would be a risk taker and innovative (*learning*), and one who was hard-driving and competitive (*authority*). After considerable deliberation, the board chose the highly competitive leader with the *authority* style. Soon afterward an activist investor attempted a hostile takeover, and the new CEO was able to navigate through the precarious situation, keep the company independent, and simultaneously begin to restructure in preparation for growth.

In a merger, designing a new culture on the basis of complementary strengths can speed up integration and create more value over time

Mergers and acquisitions can either create or destroy value. Numerous studies have shown that cultural dynamics represent one of the greatest yet most frequently overlooked determinants of integration success and postmerger performance.

For example, senior leaders from two merging international food retailers had invested heavily in their organizations' cultures and wanted to preserve their unique strengths and distinct heritages. An assessment of the cultures revealed shared values and areas of compatibility that could provide a foundation for the combined culture, along with important differences for which leaders would have to plan: Both companies emphasized *results, caring,* and *order* and valued high-quality food, good service, treating employees fairly, and maintaining a local mindset. But one operated in a more top-down manner and scored much higher on *authority,* especially in the behavior of leaders.

Because both companies valued teamwork and investments in the local community, the leaders prioritized *caring* and *purpose.* At the same time, their strategy required that they shift from top-down *authority* to a *learning* style that would encourage innovation in new-store formats and online retailing. As one senior leader said of the strategic aspiration, "We need to dare to do things differently, not play by the old rule books."

Once they had agreed on a culture, a rigorous assessment process identified leaders at both organizations whose personal style and values would allow them to serve as bridges to and champions for it. Then a program was launched to promote cultural alignment within 30 top teams, with an emphasis on clarifying priorities, making authentic connections, and developing team norms that would bring the new culture to life.

Finally, structural elements of the new organization were redesigned with culture in mind. A model for leadership was developed that encompassed recruitment, talent assessment, training and development, performance management, reward systems, and promotions. Such design considerations are often overlooked during organizational change, but if systems and structures don't align with cultural and leadership imperatives, progress can be derailed.

In a dynamic, uncertain environment, in which organizations must be more agile, *learning* gains importance

It's not surprising that *results* is the most common culture style among all the companies we have studied. Yet during a decade of helping leaders design aspirational cultures, we have seen a clear trend toward prioritizing *learning* to promote innovation and agility as businesses respond to increasingly less predictable and more complex environments. And although *learning* ranks fourth within our broader database, small companies (200 employees or fewer) and those in newer industries (such as software, technology, and wireless equipment) accord it higher values.

Consider one Silicon Valley–based technology company we worked with. Though it had built a strong business and invested in unique technology and top engineering talent, its revenue growth was starting to decline as newer, nimbler competitors made strides in a field exploding with innovation and business model disruption. Company leaders viewed the culture as a differentiator for the business and decided to diagnose, strengthen, and evolve it. We found a culture that was intensely *results* focused, team based (*caring*), and exploratory (a combination of *enjoyment* and *learning*).

After examining the overall business strategy and gaining input from employees, leaders aimed for a culture that was even more focused on *learning* and adopted our framework as a new language for the organization in its daily work. They initiated conversations between managers and employees about how to emphasize innovation and exploration. Although it takes time to change a culture, we found that the company had made notable progress just one year later. And even as it prepared for an impending sale amid ever greater competition and consolidation, employee engagement scores were on the rise.

A strong culture can be a significant liability when it is misaligned with strategy

We studied a Europe-based industrial services organization whose industry began to experience rapid and unprecedented changes in customer expectations, regulatory demands, and competitive dynamics. The company's strategy, which had historically emphasized cost leadership, needed to shift toward greater service differentiation in response. But its strong culture presented a roadblock to success.

We diagnosed the culture as highly *results* oriented, *caring,* and *order* seeking, with a top-down emphasis on *authority.* The company's leaders decided to shape it to be much more *purpose*-driven, enabling, open, and team based, which would entail an increase in *caring* along with *learning* and *purpose* and a decrease in *authority* and *results.*

This shift was particularly challenging because the current culture had served the organization well for many years, while the industry emphasized efficiency and *results.* Most managers still viewed it as a strength and fought to preserve it, threatening success for the new strategic direction.

Cultural change is daunting for any organization, but as this company realized, it's not impossible. The CEO introduced new leadership development and team coaching programs and training opportunities that would help leaders feel more comfortable with cultural evolution. When people departed, the company carefully selected new leaders who would provide supporting values, such as *caring,* and increased the emphasis on a shared *purpose.* The benefits of this strategic and cultural shift took the form of an increasingly diverse array of integrated service offerings and strong growth, particularly in emerging markets.

Four Levers for Evolving a Culture

Unlike developing and executing a business plan, changing a company's culture is inextricable from the emotional and social dynamics of people in the organization. We have found that four practices in particular lead to successful culture change:

Articulate the aspiration

Much like defining a new strategy, creating a new culture should begin with an analysis of the current one, using a framework that can be openly discussed throughout the organization. Leaders must understand what outcomes the culture produces and how it does or doesn't align with current and anticipated market and business conditions. For example, if the company's primary culture styles are *results* and *authority* but it exists in a rapidly changing industry, shifting toward *learning* or *enjoyment* (while maintaining a focus on *results*) may be appropriate.

An aspirational culture suggests the high-level principles that guide organizational initiatives, as at the technology company that sought to boost agility and flexibility amid increasing competition. Change might be framed in terms of real and present business challenges and opportunities as well as aspirations and trends. Because of culture's somewhat ambiguous and hidden nature, referring to tangible problems, such as market pressures or the challenges of growth, helps people better understand and connect to the need for change.

Select and develop leaders who align with the target culture

Leaders serve as important catalysts for change by encouraging it at all levels and creating a safe climate and what Edgar Schein calls "practice fields." Candidates for recruitment should be evaluated on their alignment with the target. A single model that can assess both organizational culture and individual leadership styles is critical for this activity.

Incumbent leaders who are unsupportive of desired change can be engaged and re-energized through training and education about the important relationship between culture and strategic direction. Often they will support the change after they understand its relevance, its anticipated benefits, and the impact that they personally can have on moving the organization toward the aspiration. However, culture change can and does lead to turnover: Some people move on because they feel they are no longer a good fit for the organization, and others are asked to leave if they jeopardize needed evolution.

Use organizational conversations about culture to underscore the importance of change

To shift the shared norms, beliefs, and implicit understandings within an organization, colleagues can talk one another through the change. Our integrated culture framework can be used to discuss current and desired culture styles and also differences in how senior leaders operate. As employees start to recognize that their leaders are talking about new business outcomes—innovation instead of quarterly earnings, for example—they will begin to behave differently themselves, creating a positive feedback loop.

Various kinds of organizational conversations, such as road shows, listening tours, and structured group discussion, can support change. Social media platforms encourage conversations between senior managers and frontline employees. Influential change champions can advocate for a culture shift through their language and actions. The technology company made a meaningful change in its culture and employee engagement by creating a structured framework for dialogue and cultivating widespread discussion.

Reinforce the desired change through organizational design

When a company's structures, systems, and processes are aligned and support the aspirational culture and strategy, instigating new culture styles and behaviors will become far easier. For example, performance management can be used to encourage employees to embody aspirational cultural attributes. Training practices can reinforce the target culture as the organization grows and adds new people. The degree of centralization and the number of hierarchical levels in the organizational structure can be adjusted to reinforce behaviors inherent to the aspirational culture. Leading scholars such as Henry Mintzberg have shown how organizational structure and other design features can have a profound impact over time on how people think and behave within an organization.

Putting It All Together

All four levers came together at a traditional manufacturer that was trying to become a full solutions provider. The change started with reformulating the strategy and was reinforced by a major brand campaign. But the president understood that the company's culture represented the biggest barrier to change and that the top leaders were the greatest lever for evolving the culture.

The culture was characterized by a drive for *results* followed by *caring* and *purpose,* the last of which was unusually strong for the industry. One employee described the company as "a talented and committed group of people focused on doing good for the planet, with genuine desire, support, and encouragement to make a difference in the community." Whereas the broader culture was highly collaborative, with flat decision making, leaders were seen as top-down, hierarchical, and sometimes political, which discouraged risk taking.

The top leaders reviewed their culture's strengths and the gaps in their own styles and discussed what was needed to achieve their strategic aspirations. They agreed that they needed more risk taking and autonomy and less hierarchy and centralized decision making. The president restructured the leadership team around strong business line leaders, freeing up time to become a better advocate for the culture and to focus more on customers.

The top team then invited a group of 100 middle managers into the conversation through a series of biannual leadership conferences. The first one established a platform for input, feedback, and the cocreation of an organizational change plan with clear cultural priorities. The president organized these managers into teams focused on critical business challenges. Each team was required to go outside the company to source ideas, to develop solutions, and to present its findings to the group for feedback. This initiative placed middle managers in change roles that would traditionally have been filled by vice presidents, giving them greater autonomy in fostering a *learning*-based culture. The intent was to create real benefits for the business while evolving the culture.

The president also initiated a program to identify employees who had positive disruptive ideas and working styles. These people were put on project teams that addressed key innovation priorities. The teams immediately began improving business results, both in core commercial metrics and in culture and engagement. After only one year employee engagement scores jumped a full 10 points, and customer Net Promoter Scores reached an all-time high—providing strong client references for the company's new and innovative solutions.

It is possible—in fact, vital—to improve organizational performance through culture change, using the simple but powerful models and methods in this article. First leaders must become aware of the culture that operates in their organization. Next they can define an aspirational target culture. Finally they can master the core change practices of articulation of the aspiration, leadership alignment, organizational conversation, and organizational design. Leading with culture may be among the few sources of sustainable competitive advantage left to companies today. Successful leaders will stop regarding culture with frustration and instead use it as a fundamental management tool.

What's Your Organization's Cultural Profile?

Before you begin an initiative to shape your organization's culture, it's important to explore where it is today. This worksheet and the questions that follow can help you formulate a preliminary assessment of your culture and get the conversation started.

Consider how your organization currently operates, what is valued, how people behave, and what unifies them. Partner with a colleague and independently rate each statement according to how well it describes your organization.

Add the two ratings in each row and then rank the eight styles. The higher the total, the stronger the match.

Compare your rankings with your colleague's and discuss the following questions:

- What do you like most about the current culture?
- What behaviors and mindsets might you evolve?
- How effective are your organization's leaders at role modeling the culture?
- What are the characteristics of people who are most successful in your culture?
- When new people don't succeed in your culture, what is the most common reason?

On a scale of 1–5, rate how well each of these statements describes your organization

1 = Not at all well, 2 = Not very well, 3 = Somewhat well, 4 = Very well, 5 = Extremely well

The organization is focused on:					The organization feels like:					Total
Collaboration and mutual trust					A big family					Caring
1	2	3	4	5	1	2	3	4	5	
Compassion and tolerance					An idealistic community or cause					Purpose
1	2	3	4	5	1	2	3	4	5	
Exploration and creativity					A dynamic project					Learning
1	2	3	4	5	1	2	3	4	5	
Fun and excitement					A celebration					Enjoyment
1	2	3	4	5	1	2	3	4	5	
Achievement and winning					A meritocracy					Results
1	2	3	4	5	1	2	3	4	5	
Strength and boldness					A competitive arena					Authority
1	2	3	4	5	1	2	3	4	5	
Planning and caution					A meticulously planned operation					Safety
1	2	3	4	5	1	2	3	4	5	
Structure and stability					A smoothly running machine					Order
1	2	3	4	5	1	2	3	4	5	

To see an expanded version of the assessment, go to this article at HBR.org.

How to Shape Your Culture

First you must identify culture targets. The best ones have some attributes in common: They align with the company's strategic direction; they're important to execute; and they reflect the demands of the external business environment. A good target should be both specific and achievable. For example, "We value our customers" can create ambiguity and lead to inconsistent choices regarding hiring, developing leaders, and running the company. A better version might be "We build genuine and positive relationships with customers; we serve our customers with humility; and we act as ambassadors for our rich brand heritage."

To Set a Culture Target:

Understand the current culture

Examine your culture—the company's founding and heritage, its espoused values, subcultures, leadership style, and team dynamics. (Use the preceding figure to start the conversation.)

Identify your culture's strengths and examine its impact on your organization today. Interview key stakeholders and influential members of the organization as needed.

Consider strategy and the environment

Assess current and future external conditions and strategic choices and determine which cultural styles will need to be strengthened or diminished in response.

Formulate a culture target according to which styles will support future changes.

Frame the aspiration in business realities

Translate the target into organizational change priorities. It should be framed not as a culture change initiative but in terms of real-world problems to be solved and solutions that create value.

Focus on *leadership alignment, organizational conversations,* and *organizational design* as the levers to guide the culture's evolution.

One Company's Experience

One large company used its search for a new director as an opportunity to bridge a problematic gap between the company's culture and the board's culture. To accomplish this, the leadership first diagnosed the two cultures along with its aspirations for the new director.

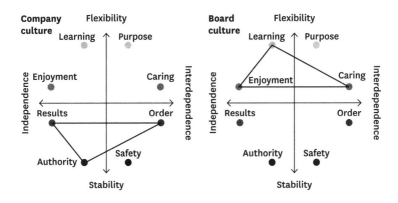

Whereas the company was highly *results* oriented and focused on *order*, discipline, and execution, the board was far more *learning* oriented, exploratory, inquisitive, and focused on *enjoyment*. A director who was *results* driven and curious would help bridge the two cultures.

Two years after an individual with the desired style was brought in, the board and the management team reported more-effective strategic planning activities and improved company performance.

Convergence Matters

When we compared employees' views on their organization's most salient cultural attributes, two types of organizations emerged: *low convergence* (employees rarely agreed on the most important cultural attributes) and *high convergence* (views were more closely aligned). In the two examples below, each dot represents one employee.

Note that in the low-convergence organization, seven of the eight cultural attributes were cited as most important, and every quadrant is represented. That means employees viewed their company in varying and often opposite ways. Some saw a *caring* organization, for example, while others saw one that emphasized *authority.*

Why is high convergence important? Because it correlates with levels of employee engagement and customer orientation. However, if the culture you have is not the one you want, high convergence will make it harder to change.

Company A: Low convergence

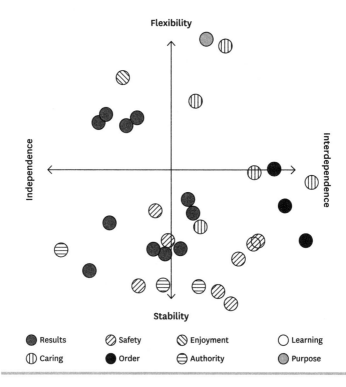

Company B: High convergence

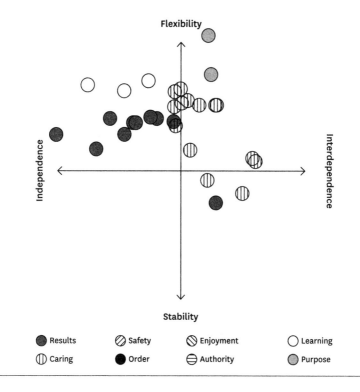

Context, Conditions, and Culture

Context matters when assessing a culture's strategic effectiveness.

Leaders must simultaneously consider culture styles and key organizational and market conditions if they want their culture to help drive performance. Region and industry are among the most germane external factors to keep in mind; critical internal considerations include alignment with strategy, leadership, and organizational design.

Region

The values of the national and regional cultures in which a company is embedded can influence patterns of behavior within the organization. (This linkage has been explored in depth by Geert Hofstede and the authors of the GLOBE study.) We find, for example, that companies operating in countries characterized by a high degree of institutional collectivism (defined as valuing equity within groups and encouraging the collective distribution of resources), such as France and Brazil, have cultures that emphasize *order* and *safety*. Companies operating in countries with low levels of uncertainty avoidance (that is, they are open to ambiguity and future uncertainty), such as the United States and Australia, place a greater emphasis on *learning, purpose,* and *enjoyment*. Such external influences are important considerations when working across borders or designing an appropriate organizational culture.

Industry

Varying cultural attributes may be needed to address industry-specific regulations and customer needs. A comparison of organizations across industries reveals evidence that cultures might adapt to meet the demands of industry environments.

Organizational cultures in financial services are more likely to emphasize *safety*. Given the increasingly complex regulations enacted in response to the financial crisis, careful work and risk management are more critical than ever in this industry. In contrast, nonprofits are far more purpose-driven, which can reinforce their commitment to a mission by aligning employee behavior around a common goal.

Culture styles ranked by industry

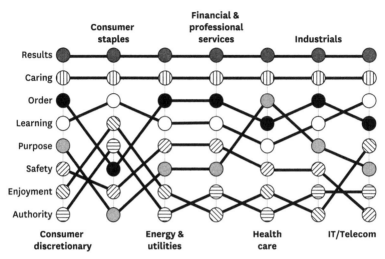

Based on an assessment of 230+ companies (industry) and a subsample of 25 companies (strategy)

Strategy

For its full benefit to be realized, a culture must support the strategic goals and plans of the business. For example, we find differences between companies that adopt a differentiation strategy and companies that pursue a cost leadership strategy. Although *results* and *caring* are key cultural characteristics at both types of companies, *enjoyment, learning,* and *purpose* are more suited to differentiation, whereas *order* and *authority* are more suited to cost leadership. Flexible cultures—which emphasize *enjoyment* and *learning*—can spur product innovation in companies aiming to differentiate themselves, whereas stable and predictable cultures, which emphasize *order* and *authority*, can help maintain operational efficiency to keep costs low.

Strategic considerations related to a company's life cycle are also linked to organizational culture. Companies with a strategy that seeks to stabilize or maintain their market position prioritize *learning*, whereas organizations operating with a turnaround strategy tend to prioritize *order* and *safety* in their efforts to redirect or reorganize unprofitable units.

Culture styles ranked by strategy

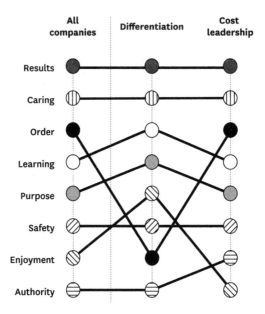

Based on an assessment of 230+ companies (industry) and a subsample of 25 companies (strategy)

Leadership

It is hard to overestimate the importance of aligning culture and leadership. The character and behaviors of a CEO and top executives can have a profound effect on culture. Conversely, culture serves to either constrain or enhance the performance of leaders. Our own data from executive recruiting activities shows that a lack of cultural fit is responsible for up to 68% of new-hire failures at the senior leadership level. For individual leaders, cultural fit is as important as capabilities and experience.

Organizational design

We see a two-way relationship between a company's culture and its particular structure. In many cases, structure and systems follow culture. For
example, companies that prioritize teamwork and collaboration might
design incentive systems that include shared team and company goals along
with rewards that recognize collective effort. However, a long-standing organizational design choice can lead to the formation of a culture. Because the
latter is far more difficult to alter, we suggest that structural changes should
be aligned with the desired culture.

About the Research

We undertook a comprehensive study of organizational culture and outcomes to explore the link between them. We analyzed the cultures of more than 230 companies along with the leadership styles and values of more than 1,300 executives across a range of industries (including consumer discretionary, consumer staples, energy and utilities, financial and professional services, health care, industrials, and IT and telecommunications), regions (Africa, Asia, Europe, the Middle East, North America, Oceania, and South America), and organizational types (public, private, and nonprofit). We diagnosed those cultures using online survey responses from approximately 25,000 employees together with interviews of company managers.

Our analysis highlighted how strongly each of the eight styles defined the organizations in our study. *Results* ranked first, and *caring* second. This pattern is consistent across company types, company sizes, regions, and industries. *Order* and *learning* ranked among the third and fourth most common styles in many cultures.

Culture appears to most directly affect employee engagement and motivation, followed by customer orientation. To model its relationship to organizational outcomes, we assessed employee engagement levels for all the companies using widely accepted survey questions and arrived at customer-orientation scores with an online questionnaire. In many cases we also documented top leaders' individual styles and values.

We found that employee engagement is most strongly related to greater flexibility, in the form of *enjoyment, learning, purpose,* and *caring.* Similarly, we observed a positive relationship between customer orientation and those four styles plus *results.* These relationships, too, are surprisingly consistent across companies. We also found that engagement and customer orientation are stronger when employees are in close agreement about the culture's characteristics.

Our research was influenced by the work of countless scholars in this field, many of whom are mentioned in this article. In addition, we stand on the shoulders of giants such as David Caldwell, Jennifer Chatman, James Heskett, John Kotter, Charles O'Reilly, and many, many others who have inspired our thinking.

Originally published in January–February 2018. Reprint R1801B

Manage Your Emotional Culture

by Sigal Barsade and Olivia A. O'Neill

BEFORE LEAVING WORK each day, employees at Ubiquity Retirement + Savings press a button in the lobby. They're not punching out—not in the traditional sense, anyway. They're actually registering their emotions. They have five buttons to choose from: a smiley face if they felt happy at work that day, a frowny face if they felt sad, and so on.

This may sound like an HR gimmick ("See? Management cares how you feel!") or an instrument of forced satisfaction ("The team with the most smiley faces wins!"). But it's neither. Ubiquity is using the data it collects to understand what motivates employees—to learn what makes them feel a sense of belonging and excitement at work. Other organizations are starting to do the same. Some use apps that record how much fun people are having. Some hire technology consultants who specialize in the monthly, weekly, daily, or even hourly tracking of moods. Unfortunately, though, these organizations are in the minority. Most companies pay little attention to how employees are—or should be—feeling. They don't realize how central emotions are to building the right culture.

When people talk about corporate culture, they're typically referring to *cognitive* culture: the shared *intellectual* values, norms, artifacts, and assumptions that serve as a guide for the group to thrive. Cognitive culture sets the tone for how employees think and behave at work—for instance, how customer-focused, innovative, team-oriented, or competitive they are or should be.

Cognitive culture is undeniably important to an organization's success. But it's only part of the story. The other critical part is what we call the group's *emotional* culture: the shared *affective* values, norms, artifacts, and assumptions that govern which emotions people have and express at work and which ones they are better off suppressing. Though the key distinction here is thinking versus feeling, the two types of culture are also transmitted differently: Cognitive culture is often conveyed verbally, whereas emotional culture tends to be conveyed through nonverbal cues such as body language and facial expression.

Despite a renaissance of scholarship (dubbed "the affective revolution") on the ways that emotions shape people's behavior at work, emotional culture is rarely managed as deliberately as cognitive culture—and often it's not managed at all. Companies suffer as a result. Employees who should be showing compassion (in health care, for example) become callous and indifferent. Teams that would benefit from joy and pride instead tolerate a culture of anger. People who lack a healthy amount of fear (say, in security firms or investment banks) act recklessly. The effects can be especially damaging during times of upheaval, such as organizational restructurings and financial downturns.

In our research over the past decade, we have found that emotional culture influences employee satisfaction, burnout, teamwork, and even hard measures such as financial performance and absenteeism. Countless empirical studies show the significant impact of emotions on how people perform on tasks, how engaged and creative they are, how committed they are to their organizations, and how they make decisions. Positive emotions are consistently associated with better performance, quality, and customer service—this holds true across roles and industries and at various organizational levels. On the flip side (with certain short-term exceptions), negative emotions such as group anger, sadness, fear, and the like usually lead to negative outcomes, including poor performance and high turnover.

Idea in Brief

The Problem

Most companies pay little attention to their emotional culture—which feelings people have (and should have) at work, and which ones they keep to themselves. That presents problems for both individuals and organizations.

The Reason

Research shows that, for better or worse, emotions influence employees' commitment, creativity, decision making, work quality, and likelihood of sticking around—and you can see the effects on the bottom line. So it's important to monitor and manage people's feelings as deliberately as you do their mindset.

The Solution

Once you have a handle on your existing emotional culture, you can shape it in several ways. Explicitly say which emotions will help the organization thrive, channel the feelings that people have and express naturally, and cultivate the ones you want through emotional contagion and the power of "deep acting."

So when managers ignore emotional culture, they're glossing over a vital part of what makes people—and organizations—tick. They may understand its importance in theory but can still shy away from emotions at work. Leaders expect to influence how people think and behave on the job, but they may feel ill equipped to understand and actively manage how employees feel and express their emotions at work. Or they may regard doing so as irrelevant, not part of their job, or unprofessional.

In our interviews with executives and employees, some people have told us that their organizations lack emotion altogether. But every organization has an emotional culture, even if it's one of suppression. By not only allowing emotions into the workplace, but also understanding and consciously shaping them, leaders can better motivate their employees. In this article we'll illustrate some of the ways in which emotional culture manifests at work and the impact it can have in a range of settings, from health care and emergency services to finance, consulting, and high tech. Drawing on our findings, we'll also suggest ways of creating and maintaining an emotional culture that will help you achieve your company's larger goals.

Delving Beneath the Surface

Some companies have begun to explicitly include emotions in their management principles. For instance, PepsiCo, Southwest Airlines, Whole Foods Market, The Container Store, and Zappos all list love or caring among their corporate values. Similarly, C&S Wholesale Grocers, Camden Property Trust, Cisco Finance, Ubiquity, and Vail Resorts, along with many start-ups, highlight the importance of fun to their success.

But to get a comprehensive read on an organization's emotional culture and then deliberately manage it, you have to make sure that what is codified in mission statements and on corporate badges is also enacted in the "micromoments" of daily organizational life. These consist of small gestures rather than bold declarations of feeling. For example, little acts of kindness and support can add up to an emotional culture characterized by caring and compassion.

Facial expressions and body language are equally powerful. If a manager consistently comes to work looking angry (whether he means to or not), he may cultivate a culture of anger. This phenomenon is surprisingly common: In one study, Don Gibson, the dean and a professor of management at Fairfield University's Dolan School of Business, found that working professionals from multiple organizations actually felt more comfortable expressing anger than joy on the job (they reported expressing anger three times as often). You can imagine the ripple effects.

Office décor and furnishings, too, may suggest what's expected or appropriate emotionally. Photos of employees laughing at social events or action figures perched on cubicle walls can signal a culture of joy. Signs with lists of rules and consequences for breaking them can reflect a culture of fear. Comfy chairs and tissues in small conference rooms convey that it's OK to bare your soul or cry if you need to.

But as Edgar Schein, a professor emeritus at MIT's Sloan School, has shown with his popular "three levels of culture" model, the most deeply entrenched elements of organizational culture are the least visible. Take, for instance, the deep underlying assumption that pitting employees against one another gets the best work out of them.

That's not the kind of thing managers publicize; sometimes they're even unaware that they are fostering this dynamic. And yet it's felt by leaders and employees alike. While it may result in healthy competition, it's just as likely to create a strong culture of envy, which can erode trust and undermine employees' ability to collaborate.

Emotional Cultures in Action

Nearly 30 years ago the social psychologist Phil Shaver and his colleagues found that people can reliably distinguish among 135 emotions. But understanding the most basic ones—joy, love, anger, fear, sadness—is a good place to start for any leader trying to manage an emotional culture. Here are a few examples to illustrate how these emotions can play out in organizations.

A culture of joy
Let's begin with one that's often clearly articulated and actively reinforced by management—above the surface and easy to spot. Vail Resorts recognizes that cultivating joy among employees helps customers have fun too, which matters a lot in the hospitality business. It also gives the organization an edge in retaining top talent in an extremely competitive industry. "Have fun" is listed as a company value and modeled by Vail's CEO, Rob Katz—who, for instance, had ice water dumped on his head during a corporate ALS Ice Bucket Challenge and then jumped fully clothed into a pool. About 250 executives and other employees followed his lead.

This playful spirit at the top permeates Vail. Management tactics, special outings, celebrations, and rewards all support the emotional culture. Resort managers consistently model joy and prescribe it for their teams. During the workday they give out pins when they notice employees spontaneously having fun or helping others enjoy their jobs. Rather than asking people to follow standardized customer service scripts, they tell everyone to "go out there and have fun." Mark Gasta, the company's chief people officer, says he regularly sees ski-lift operators dancing, making jokes, doing "whatever it takes to have fun and entertain the guest" while ensuring a safe experience

Tracking emotions

Companies have started using apps like Niko Niko to help individual employees and teams log their emotional reaction to various activities and make the connection between their moods and productivity.

on the slopes. On a day-to-day basis, Vail encourages employees to collaborate, because, as Gasta points out, "leaving people out is not fun." At an annual ceremony, a Have Fun award goes to whoever led that year's best initiative promoting fun at work. The resort also fosters off-the-job joy with "first tracks" (first access to the ski slopes for employees), adventure trips, and frequent social gatherings.

All this is in service to an emotional culture that makes intuitive sense. (Joy at a ski resort? Of course.) But now consider an organization where the demand for joy wasn't immediately visible. When we surveyed employees at Cisco Finance about their organization's emotional culture, it became clear to management that fostering joy should be a priority. The survey didn't ask employees how they felt at work; it asked them what emotions they saw their coworkers expressing on a regular basis. (By having employees report on colleagues' emotions, researchers could obtain a more objective, bird's-eye view of the culture.) It turned out that joy was one of the strongest drivers of employee satisfaction and commitment at the company—and more of it was needed to keep up engagement.

So management made joy an explicit cultural value, calling it "Pause for Fun." This signaled that it was an important outcome to track— just like productivity, creativity, and other elements of performance. Many companies use annual employee engagement surveys to gauge joy in the abstract, often in the form of job satisfaction and commitment to the organization. But Cisco Finance measured it much more specifically and is conducting follow-up surveys to track whether it is actually increasing. In addition, leaders throughout the organization support this cultural value with their own behavior—for example, by creating humorous videos that show them pausing for fun.

A culture of companionate love

Another emotion we've examined extensively—one that's common in life but rarely mentioned by name in organizations—is companionate love. This is the degree of affection, caring, and compassion that employees feel and express toward one another.

In a 16-month study of a large long-term-care facility on the East Coast, we found that workers in units with strong cultures of companionate love had lower absenteeism, less burnout, and greater teamwork and job satisfaction than their colleagues in other units. Employees also performed their work better, as demonstrated by more-satisfied patients, better patient moods, and fewer unnecessary trips to the emergency room. (Employees whose dispositions were positive to begin with received an extra performance boost from the culture.) The families of patients in units with stronger cultures of companionate love reported higher satisfaction with the facility. These results show a powerful connection between emotional culture and business performance.

Because this study took place in a health care setting, we wondered whether companionate love matters only in "helping" industries. So we surveyed more than 3,200 employees in 17 organizations spanning seven industries: biopharmaceutical, engineering, financial services, higher education, public utilities, real estate, and travel.

In organizations where employees felt and expressed companionate love toward one another, people reported greater job satisfaction, commitment, and personal accountability for work performance.

Take Censeo, a consulting firm that has deliberately cultivated a culture of companionate love. Cofounder and CEO Raj Sharma wanted to build a company that made authentic connections with clients. Along the way, Sharma realized that this strategy, which increased clients' trust and the firm's impact, was also critical to Censeo's organizational culture.

Now the firm hires people who will help sustain its culture; that means turning away some really smart people who would destroy it. Censeo also encourages employees to cultivate genuine relationships by interacting socially both at and outside work. The message seems to be getting through: When asked to describe colleagues at the firm, one junior analyst called them "my friends." Employees also hold themselves accountable for treating one another with compassion. They'll confront colleagues—including those above them in the hierarchy—for blatantly disregarding the feelings of others or frequently blowing up at coworkers.

A culture of fear

Of course, organizations can be defined by negative emotions as well. In *Turn the Ship Around!* the retired Navy captain L. David Marquet describes how a culture of fear plagued the USS *Santa Fe,* a nuclear submarine that suffered under extreme command-and-control leadership before he took over. The crew had low morale and the worst retention rate in the fleet.

Nuclear submarines must accomplish their missions while maintaining security and safety, so performance depends in large part on the skill and judgment of the crew. Marquet argues that the constant fear of being yelled at—for making mistakes, not knowing things, challenging authority, and so on—made it harder for sailors to think well and act quickly. This view is backed by research that the Berkeley professor emeritus Barry Staw and his colleagues have done on "threat rigidity" (the tendency to narrow one's focus under threat) and by findings on the impact of excessive stress on the prefrontal cortex: It impairs executive functions such as judgment, memory, and impulse control.

Marquet changed that emotional culture by using classic "high involvement" management techniques, such as empowering crew members to make decisions and not punishing them for every misstep. As a result, they became more confident and accountable—and less inclined to simply wait for permission or directions from their commanding officer. The transformation paid off. Marquet led the ship from low-performing to award-winning, and 10 of his top 20 officers later went on to become submarine captains.

What Happens When Emotions Intersect

Clearly, fear can be toxic, but even positive emotions can have unintended side effects if given too much sway. In a culture of unmitigated joy, fun might impede work. In a culture of love, where everyone feels like family, employees might struggle to have honest conversations about problems. To quote one person we interviewed, "People don't want to talk about conflict because they don't want to get in the way of the love."

Sometimes organizations avoid those problems because multiple emotions balance one another out. For example, in a comprehensive study of firefighters' organizational culture (conducted by one of us, Olivia O'Neill, and Nancy Rothbard, a professor at Wharton), two emotions came through quite strongly. Participants described a culture of joviality, expressed mainly through elaborate jokes and pranks. (They said their most important rule for hiring someone new was "No stiffs.") But that coexisted with a culture of companionate love, which the researchers hadn't expected to see in a typically masculine profession. The firefighters supported one another emotionally—offering words of encouragement when someone was struggling after a tough call, for example, or was going through a painful divorce. They also offered nonverbal gestures of affection, such as a bear hug for someone who was choked up over a personal issue.

There were reasons for both emotional cultures to be strong: Joviality helped teams coordinate better on the job, because all the pranks had honed their understanding of individuals' weaknesses (anthropologists would call this an evolutionary advantage of play). Monitoring and managing those weaknesses is particularly important in fast-moving, high-stress, or dangerous situations. And companionate love helped the firefighters heal from the traumatic events endemic in their jobs.

Like any other emotion, companionate love can lead to varying outcomes, depending on what it's paired with. For the firefighters, it had a tempering effect on the joviality and teasing, which—if taken to extremes—could become isolating and hurtful.

Another example of how emotions intersect comes from our research with the Católica-Lisbon professor Francesco Sguera. In a study of a major medical center in the United States, we found that the emotional culture was largely defined by anxiety and anger. The medical center's punishment-based "point system" reinforced the anxiety: "If you call in sick, you get a point," an employee wrote. "If you are one minute late for work, you get a point. We often feel that we are liabilities to the department, as disposable as gauze." The rampant anxiety led to many negative outcomes, including poor financial performance, burnout, and low job satisfaction. However, in units where a strong culture of anxiety was coupled with companionate love, employee performance and attitudes matched those in units with lower anxiety. The culture of companionate love essentially served as an antidote to the culture of anxiety. It reduced the negative impact on the bottom line—specifically, on gross profit margin—by offsetting the ill effects on employee attitudes and behavior. Although employees expressed a lot of anxiety and saw it all around them, knowing that they were cared for by their colleagues helped them to deal with it.

Creating an Emotional Culture

To cultivate a particular emotional culture, you'll need to get people to feel the emotions valued by the organization or team—or at least to behave as if they do. Here are three effective methods:

Harness what people already feel

Some employees will experience the desired emotions quite naturally. This can happen in isolated moments of compassion or gratitude, for example. When such feelings arise regularly, that's a sign you're building the culture you want. If people have them periodically and need help sustaining them, you can try incorporating some gentle nudges during the workday. You might schedule some time for meditation, for instance; or provide mindfulness apps on people's work devices to remind them to simply breathe, relax, or laugh; or create a kudos board, like the one in an ICU we studied, where people can post kind words about other employees.

. But what can you do about emotions that are toxic to the culture you're striving for? How can you discourage them when they already exist? Expecting people to "put a lid" on those feelings is both ineffective and destructive; the emotions will just come out later in counterproductive ways. It's important to listen when employees express their concerns so that they feel they are being heard. That's not to say you should encourage venting, or just let the emotions flow with no attempt at solving the root problems. Indeed, research shows that extended venting can lead to poor outcomes. You're better off helping employees think about situations in a more constructive way. For example, loneliness, which can eat away at employee attitudes and performance, is best addressed through cognitive reappraisal—getting people to reexamine their views of others' actions. Considering plausible benign motivations for their colleagues' behavior will make them less likely to fixate on negative explanations that could send them into a spiral.

Model the emotions you want to cultivate

A long line of research on emotional contagion shows that people in groups "catch" feelings from others through behavioral mimicry and subsequent changes in brain function. If you regularly walk into a room smiling with high energy, you're much more likely to create a culture of joy than if you wear a neutral expression. Your employees will smile back and start to mean it.

Cultural Artifacts

AN ORGANIZATION'S PHYSICAL ENVIRONMENT can send cues—subtle or strong—about which feelings employees do and should express at work. Here are some examples:

1

2

3

1. This coworking space for technology start-ups reflects a culture of joy and fun. Note the robo-cocktail posters and drones parked on the wall.

2. An intensive care unit at one university hospital has a culture of fear: Employees must stay silent so as not to disturb critically ill patients.

3. But fear and sadness in the ICU are mitigated by companionate love, reflected in this "kudos" board for employees.

But negative feelings, too, spread like wildfire. If you frequently express frustration, that emotion will infect your team members, and their team members, and so on throughout the organization. Before you know it, you'll have created a culture of frustration.

So consciously model the emotions you want to cultivate in your company. Some organizations go a step further and explicitly ask employees to spread certain emotions. Ubiquity Retirement + Savings says, "Inspire happiness with contagious enthusiasm. Own your joy and lend it out." Vail Resorts says, "Enjoy your work and share the contagious spirit."

Get people to fake it till they feel it

If employees don't experience the desired emotion at a particular moment, they can still help maintain their organization's emotional culture. That's because people express emotions both spontaneously and strategically at work. Social psychology research has long shown that individuals tend to conform to group norms of emotional expression, imitating others out of a desire to be liked and accepted. So employees in a strong emotional culture who would not otherwise feel and express the valued emotion will begin to demonstrate it—even if their initial motivation is to be compliant rather than to internalize the culture.

This benefits the organization, not just the individuals trying to thrive in it. In early anthropological studies of group rituals, strategic emotional expression was found to facilitate group cohesion by overpowering individual feelings and synchronizing interpersonal behavior.

So maintaining the appropriate culture sometimes entails disregarding what you are truly feeling. Through "surface acting," employees can display the valued emotion without even wanting to feel it. Surface acting isn't a long-term solution, though. Research shows that it can eventually lead to burnout—particularly in the absence of any outlet for authentic emotions.

A better way to cultivate a desired emotion is through "deep acting." With this technique, people make a focused effort to feel a certain way, and then suddenly they do. Imagine that an employee at an accounting firm has a family emergency and requests a week off work at the height of tax audit season. Although his boss's first thought is *No—not now—no!* she could engage in deep acting to change her immediate feelings of justifiable panic into genuine caring and concern for her subordinate. By trying hard to empathize, saying "Of course you should go be with your family!" and using the same facial expressions, body language, and tone of voice she would use when actually feeling those emotions, she could coax herself into the real thing. She would also be modeling a desired behavior for the subordinate and the rest of the team.

Fortunately, all these ways of creating an emotional culture—whether they involve really feeling the emotion or simply acting that way—can reinforce one another and strengthen the culture's norms. People don't have to put on an act forever. Those who begin by expressing an emotion out of a desire to conform will start to actually feel it through emotional contagion. They'll also receive positive reinforcement for following the norms, which will make them more likely to demonstrate the emotion again.

Of course, the culture will be much stronger and more likely to endure if people truly believe in the values and assumptions behind it. Someone who is uncomfortable with an organization's emotional culture and has to keep pretending in order to be successful would probably be better off moving to a different work environment. Companies often have more than one emotional culture, so another unit or department might be a good fit. But if the culture is homogeneous, the employee may want to leave the company entirely.

Implementation Matters at All Levels

Just like other aspects of organizational culture, emotional culture should be supported at all levels of the organization. The role of top management is to drive it.

Leaders are often insufficiently aware of how much influence they have in creating an emotional culture. Traci Fenton is the founder and CEO of WorldBlu, a consulting firm that tackles fear at work. She shares this example: At one *Fortune* 500 company, unbeknownst to the CEO, senior employees regularly use text message codes to describe his nonverbal expressions of anger in meetings. "RED" means he is getting red in the face. "VEIN" means his veins are popping out. "ACP," which stands for "assume the crash position," means he is about to start throwing things. This leader is very effective at creating an emotional culture—but it's probably not the one he wants.

So don't underestimate the importance of day-to-day modeling. Large, symbolic emotional gestures are powerful, but only if they are in line with daily behavior. Senior executives can also shape an emotional culture through organizational practices. Take "compassionate firing," which is common at companies that build a strong culture of companionate love. Carlos Gutierrez, the vice president of R&D systems at Lattice Semiconductor, was deeply concerned about the impact of layoffs on his employees. He recognized that the traditional HR protocol of asking terminated employees to clean out their desks immediately and leave the premises would be especially painful to people who had worked side by side for 10 to 20 years. Along with his partners in HR and R&D, he implemented a protocol whereby employees had an extended time to say good-bye to their colleagues and to commemorate their time together at the company. Also, although two-thirds of the R&D workforce is outside the United States, Sherif Sweha, the corporate vice president of R&D, believed it was important for the affected team members in each region to receive the news from a senior leader face-to-face. So he and members of his staff flew to the company's sites in Asia to have in-person conversations with all the employees to be laid off—and also those who would remain with the company.

Though top management sets the first example and establishes the formal rules, middle managers and frontline supervisors ensure that the emotional values are consistently practiced by others. Because one of the biggest influences on employees is their immediate boss, the suggestions that apply to senior executives also apply to those managers: They should ensure that the emotions they express at work reflect the chosen culture, and they should speak explicitly about what is expected from employees.

It's also important to link the emotional culture to operations and processes, including performance management systems. At Vail Resorts the culture of joy has been incorporated into the annual review, which indicates how well each employee integrates fun into the work environment and rates everyone on supporting behaviors, such as being inclusive, welcoming, approachable, and positive. Someone who exceeds expectations is described as not only taking part in the fun but also offering "recommendations to improve the work environment to integrate fun."

Decades' worth of research demonstrates the importance of organizational culture, yet most of it has focused on the cognitive component. As we've shown, organizations also have an emotional pulse, and managers must track it closely to motivate their teams and reach their goals.

Emotional culture is shaped by how all employees—from the highest echelons to the front lines—comport themselves day in and day out. But it's up to senior leaders to establish which emotions will help the organization thrive, model those emotions, and reward others for doing the same. Companies in which they do this have a lot to gain.

Originally published in January–February 2016. Reprint R1601C

The Neuroscience of Trust

by Paul J. Zak

COMPANIES ARE TWISTING THEMSELVES into knots to empower and challenge their employees. They're anxious about the sad state of engagement, and rightly so, given the value they're losing. Consider Gallup's meta-analysis of decades' worth of data: It shows that high engagement—defined largely as having a strong connection with one's work and colleagues, feeling like a real contributor, and enjoying ample chances to learn—consistently leads to positive outcomes for both individuals and organizations. The rewards include higher productivity, better-quality products, and increased profitability.

So it's clear that creating an employee-centric culture can be good for business. But how do you do that effectively? Culture is typically designed in an ad hoc way around random perks like gourmet meals or "karaoke Fridays," often in thrall to some psychological fad. And despite the evidence that you can't buy higher job satisfaction, organizations still use golden handcuffs to keep good employees in place. While such efforts might boost workplace happiness in the short term, they fail to have any lasting effect on talent retention or performance.

In my research I've found that building a culture of trust is what makes a meaningful difference. Employees in high-trust organizations are more productive, have more energy at work, collaborate better with their colleagues, and stay with their employers longer than people working at low-trust companies. They also suffer less chronic stress and are happier with their lives, and these factors fuel stronger performance.

Leaders understand the stakes—at least in principle. In its 2016 global CEO survey, PwC reported that 55% of CEOs think that a lack of trust is a threat to their organization's growth. But most have done little to increase trust, mainly because they aren't sure where to start. In this article I provide a science-based framework that will help them.

About a decade ago, in an effort to understand how company culture affects performance, I began measuring the brain activity of people while they worked. The neuroscience experiments I have run reveal eight ways that leaders can effectively create and manage a culture of trust. I'll describe those strategies and explain how some organizations are using them to good effect. But first, let's look at the science behind the framework.

What's Happening in the Brain

Back in 2001 I derived a mathematical relationship between trust and economic performance. Though my paper on this research described the social, legal, and economic environments that cause differences in trust, I couldn't answer the most basic question: Why do two people trust each other in the first place? Experiments around the world have shown that humans are naturally inclined to trust others—but don't always. I hypothesized that there must be a neurologic signal that indicates when we should trust someone. So I started a long-term research program to see if that was true.

I knew that in rodents a brain chemical called oxytocin had been shown to signal that another animal was safe to approach. I wondered if that was the case in humans, too. No one had looked into it, so I decided to investigate. To measure trust and its reciprocation (trustworthiness) objectively, my team used a strategic decision task developed by researchers in the lab of Vernon Smith, a Nobel laureate in economics. In our experiment, a participant chooses an amount of money to send to a stranger via computer, knowing that

Idea in Brief

The Problem

Leaders know that low employee engagement is a sign of lost value—it's clearly something they want to fix. But most of them don't know how, so they provide random perks, hoping those will move the needle.

The Solution

It's much more effective to create a culture of trust. Neuroscience research shows that you can do this through eight key management behaviors that stimulate the production of oxytocin, a brain chemical that facilitates teamwork.

The Payoff

By fostering organizational trust, you can increase employees' productivity and energy levels, improve collaboration, and cultivate a happier, more loyal workforce.

the money will triple in amount and understanding that the recipient may or may not share the spoils. Therein lies the conflict: The recipient can either keep all the cash or be trustworthy and share it with the sender.

To measure oxytocin levels during the exchange, my colleagues and I developed a protocol to draw blood from people's arms before and immediately after they made decisions to trust others (if they were senders) or to be trustworthy (if they were receivers). Because we didn't want to influence their behavior, we didn't tell participants what the study was about, even though there was no way they could consciously control how much oxytocin they produced. We found that the more money people received (denoting greater trust on the part of senders), the more oxytocin their brains produced. And the amount of oxytocin recipients produced predicted how trustworthy—that is, how likely to share the money—they would be.

Since the brain generates messaging chemicals all the time, it was possible we had simply observed random changes in oxytocin. To prove that it *causes* trust, we safely administered doses of synthetic oxytocin into living human brains (through a nasal spray). Comparing participants who received a real dose with those who received a placebo, we found that giving people 24 IU of synthetic oxytocin

How Trust Creates Joy

EXPERIMENTS SHOW THAT HAVING A SENSE of higher purpose stimulates oxytocin production, as does trust. Trust and purpose then mutually reinforce each other, providing a mechanism for extended oxytocin release, which produces happiness.

So, joy on the job comes from doing purpose-driven work with a trusted team. In the nationally representative data set described in the main article, the correlation between (1) trust reinforced by purpose and (2) joy is very high: 0.77. It means that joy can be considered a "sufficient statistic" that reveals how effectively your company's culture engages employees. To measure this, simply ask, "How much do you enjoy your job on a typical day?"

more than doubled the amount of money they sent to a stranger. Using a variety of psychological tests, we showed that those receiving oxytocin remained cognitively intact. We also found that they did not take excessive risks in a gambling task, so the increase in trust was not due to neural disinhibition. Oxytocin appeared to do just one thing—reduce the fear of trusting a stranger.

My group then spent the next 10 years running additional experiments to identify the promoters and inhibitors of oxytocin. This research told us why trust varies across individuals and situations. For example, high stress is a potent oxytocin inhibitor. (Most people intuitively know this: When they are stressed out, they do not interact with others effectively.) We also discovered that oxytocin increases a person's empathy, a useful trait for social creatures trying to work together. We were starting to develop insights that could be used to design high-trust cultures, but to confirm them, we had to get out of the lab.

So we obtained permission to run experiments at numerous field sites where we measured oxytocin and stress hormones and then assessed employees' productivity and ability to innovate. This research even took me to the rain forest of Papua New Guinea, where I measured oxytocin in indigenous people to see if the relationship between oxytocin and trust is universal. (It is.) Drawing on all these findings, I created a survey instrument that quantifies trust within organizations by measuring its constituent factors (described in the next section). That survey has allowed me to study several thousand companies and develop a framework for managers.

How to Manage for Trust

Through the experiments and the surveys, I identified eight management behaviors that foster trust. These behaviors are measurable and can be managed to improve performance.

Recognize excellence

The neuroscience shows that recognition has the largest effect on trust when it occurs immediately after a goal has been met, when it comes from peers, and when it's tangible, unexpected, personal, and public. Public recognition not only uses the power of the crowd to celebrate successes but also inspires others to aim for excellence. And it gives top performers a forum for sharing best practices, so others can learn from them.

Barry-Wehmiller Companies, a supplier of manufacturing and technology services, is a high-trust organization that effectively recognizes top performers in the 80 production-automation manufacturers it owns. CEO Bob Chapman and his team started a program in which employees at each plant nominate an outstanding peer annually. The winner is kept secret until announced to everyone, and the facility is closed on the day of the celebration. The chosen employee's family and close friends are invited to attend (without tipping off the winner), and the entire staff joins them. Plant leaders kick off the ceremony by reading the nominating letters about the winner's contributions and bring it to a close with a favorite perk—the keys to a sports car the winner gets to drive for a week. Though the recognition isn't immediate, it is tangible, unexpected, and both personal and public. And by having employees help pick the winners, Barry-Wehmiller gives everyone, not just the people at the top, a say in what constitutes excellence. All this seems to be working well for the company: It has grown from a single plant in 1987 to a conglomerate that brings in $2.4 billion in annual revenue today.

Induce "challenge stress"

When a manager assigns a team a difficult but achievable job, the moderate stress of the task releases neurochemicals, including oxytocin and adrenocorticotropin, that intensify people's focus and strengthen social connections. When team members need to work together to reach a goal, brain activity coordinates their behaviors efficiently. But this works only if challenges are attainable and have a concrete end point; vague or impossible goals cause people to give up before they even start. Leaders should check in frequently to assess progress and adjust goals that are too easy or out of reach.

The need for achievability is reinforced by Harvard Business School professor Teresa Amabile's findings on the power of progress: When Amabile analyzed 12,000 diary entries of employees from a variety of industries, she found that 76% of people reported that their best days involved making progress toward goals.

Give people discretion in how they do their work

Once employees have been trained, allow them, whenever possible, to manage people and execute projects in their own way. Being trusted to figure things out is a big motivator: A 2014 Citigroup and LinkedIn survey found that nearly half of employees would give up a 20% raise for greater control over how they work.

Autonomy also promotes innovation, because different people try different approaches. Oversight and risk management procedures can help minimize negative deviations while people experiment. And postproject debriefs allow teams to share how positive deviations came about so that others can build on their success.

Often, younger or less experienced employees will be your chief innovators, because they're less constrained by what "usually" works. That's how progress was made in self-driving cars. After five years and a significant investment by the U.S. government in the big three auto manufacturers, no autonomous military vehicles had been produced. Changing tack, the Defense Advanced Research Projects Agency offered all comers a large financial prize for a self-driving car that could complete a course in the Mojave Desert in less than 10 hours. Two years later a group of engineering students from Stanford University won the challenge—and $2 million.

Enable job crafting

When companies trust employees to choose which projects they'll work on, people focus their energies on what they care about most. As a result, organizations like the Morning Star Company—the largest producer of tomato products in the world—have highly productive colleagues who stay with the company year after year. At Morning Star (a company I've worked with), people don't even have job titles; they self-organize into work groups. Gaming software company Valve gives employees desks on wheels and encourages them to join projects that seem "interesting" and "rewarding." But they're still held accountable. Clear expectations are set when employees join a new group, and 360-degree evaluations are done when projects wrap up, so that individual contributions can be measured.

Share information broadly

Only 40% of employees report that they are well informed about their company's goals, strategies, and tactics. This uncertainty about the company's direction leads to chronic stress, which inhibits the release of oxytocin and undermines teamwork. Openness is the antidote. Organizations that share their "flight plans" with employees reduce uncertainty about where they are headed and why. Ongoing communication is key: A 2015 study of 2.5 million manager-led teams in 195 countries found that workforce engagement improved when supervisors had some form of daily communication with direct reports.

Social media optimization company Buffer goes further than most by posting its salary formula online for everyone to see. Want to know what CEO Joel Gascoigne makes? Just look it up. That's openness.

Intentionally build relationships

The brain network that oxytocin activates is evolutionarily old. This means that the trust and sociality that oxytocin enables are deeply embedded in our nature. Yet at work we often get the

The Impact of Trust in Organizations

COMPARED WITH PEOPLE AT LOW-TRUST COMPANIES, people at high-trust companies report 74% less stress, 106% more energy at work, 50% higher productivity, 13% fewer sick days, 76% more engagement, 29% more satisfaction with their lives, and 40% less burnout.

message that we should focus on completing tasks, not on making friends. Neuroscience experiments by my lab show that when people intentionally build social ties at work, their performance improves. A Google study similarly found that managers who "express interest in and concern for team members' success and personal well-being" outperform others in the quality and quantity of their work.

Yes, even engineers need to socialize. A study of software engineers in Silicon Valley found that those who connected with others and helped them with their projects not only earned the respect and trust of their peers but were also more productive themselves. You can help people build social connections by sponsoring lunches, after-work parties, and team-building activities. It may sound like forced fun, but when people care about one another, they perform better because they don't want to let their teammates down. Adding a moderate challenge to the mix (white-water rafting counts) will speed up the social-bonding process.

Facilitate whole-person growth

High-trust workplaces help people develop personally as well as professionally. Numerous studies show that acquiring new work skills isn't enough; if you're not growing as a human being, your performance will suffer. High-trust companies adopt a growth mindset when developing talent. Some even find that when managers set clear goals, give employees the autonomy to reach them, and provide consistent feedback, the backward-looking annual performance review is no longer necessary. Instead, managers and direct reports can meet more frequently to focus on professional and personal growth. This is the approach taken by

Accenture and Adobe Systems. Managers can ask questions like, "Am I helping you get your next job?" to probe professional goals. Assessing personal growth includes discussions about work-life integration, family, and time for recreation and reflection. Investing in the whole person has a powerful effect on engagement and retention.

Show vulnerability

Leaders in high-trust workplaces ask for help from colleagues instead of just telling them to do things. My research team has found that this stimulates oxytocin production in others, increasing their trust and cooperation. Asking for help is a sign of a secure leader— one who engages everyone to reach goals. Jim Whitehurst, CEO of open-source software maker Red Hat, has said, "I found that being very open about the things I did not know actually had the opposite effect than I would have thought. It helped me build credibility." Asking for help is effective because it taps into the natural human impulse to cooperate with others.

The Return on Trust

After identifying and measuring the managerial behaviors that sustain trust in organizations, my team and I tested the impact of trust on business performance. We did this in several ways. First, we gathered evidence from a dozen companies that have launched policy changes to raise trust (most were motivated by a slump in their profits or market share). Second, we conducted the field experiments mentioned earlier: In two businesses where trust varies by department, my team gave groups of employees specific tasks, gauged their productivity and innovation in those tasks, and gathered very detailed data—including direct measures of brain activity—showing that trust improves performance. And third, with the help of an independent survey firm, we collected data in February 2016 from a nationally representative sample of 1,095 working adults in the U.S. The findings from all three sources were similar, but I will focus on what we learned from the national data since it's generalizable.

By surveying the employees about the extent to which firms practiced the eight behaviors, we were able to calculate the level of trust for each organization. (To avoid priming respondents, we never used the word "trust" in surveys.) The U.S. average for organizational trust was 70% (out of a possible 100%). Fully 47% of respondents worked in organizations where trust was below the average, with one firm scoring an abysmally low 15%. Overall, companies scored lowest on recognizing excellence and sharing information (67% and 68%, respectively). So the data suggests that the average U.S. company could enhance trust by improving in these two areas—even if it didn't improve in the other six.

The effect of trust on self-reported work performance was powerful. Respondents whose companies were in the top quartile indicated they had 106% more energy and were 76% more engaged at work than respondents whose firms were in the bottom quartile. They also reported being 50% more productive—which is consistent with our objective measures of productivity from studies we have done with employees at work. Trust had a major impact on employee loyalty as well: Compared with employees at low-trust companies, 50% more of those working at high-trust organizations planned to stay with their employer over the next year, and 88% more said they would recommend their company to family and friends as a place to work.

My team also found that those working in high-trust companies enjoyed their jobs 60% more, were 70% more aligned with their companies' purpose, and felt 66% closer to their colleagues. And a high-trust culture improves how people treat one another and themselves. Compared with employees at low-trust organizations, the high-trust folks had 11% more empathy for their workmates, depersonalized them 41% less often, and experienced 40% less burnout from their work. They felt a greater sense of accomplishment, as well—41% more.

Again, this analysis supports the findings from our qualitative and scientific studies. But one new—and surprising—thing we learned is that high-trust companies pay more. Employees earn an additional $6,450 a year, or 17% more, at companies in the highest quartile of trust, compared with those in the lowest quartile. The only way this can occur in a competitive labor market is if employees in high-trust companies are more productive and innovative.

———————

Former Herman Miller CEO Max De Pree once said, "The first responsibility of a leader is to define reality. The last is to say thank you. In between the two, the leader must become a servant."

The experiments I have run strongly support this view. Ultimately, you cultivate trust by setting a clear direction, giving people what they need to see it through, and getting out of their way.

It's not about being easy on your employees or expecting less from them. High-trust companies hold people accountable but without micromanaging them. They treat people like responsible adults.

Originally published in January–February 2017.   Reprint R1701E

Creating a Purpose-Driven Organization

by Robert E. Quinn and Anjan V. Thakor

WHEN GERRY ANDERSON FIRST became the president of DTE Energy, he did not believe in the power of higher organizational purpose.

We're not talking about having a clear mission that focuses largely on how a business will generate economic value. DTE had one that set out the goal of creating long-term gains for shareholders, and Anderson understood its importance.

A higher purpose is not about economic exchanges. It reflects something more aspirational. It explains how the people involved with an organization are making a difference, gives them a sense of meaning, and draws their support. But like many of the leaders we've interviewed in our research, Anderson started his tenure as president skeptical about how much it mattered. The concept of higher purpose didn't fit into his mostly economic understanding of the firm.

But then the Great Recession of 2008 hit, and he knew he had to get his people to devote more of themselves to work. Even before the financial crisis, surveys had demonstrated that DTE employees were not very engaged. It was a classic quandary: Employees couldn't seem to break free of old, tired behaviors. They weren't bringing their smarts and creativity to their jobs. They weren't performing up to their potential. Anderson knew that he needed a more committed workforce but did not know how to get one.

That was when retired army major general Joe Robles, then the CEO of USAA and a DTE board member, invited Anderson to visit some USAA call centers. Familiar with the culture of most call centers, Anderson expected to see people going through the motions. Instead he watched positive, fully engaged employees collaborate and go the extra mile for customers. When Anderson asked how this could be, Robles answered that a leader's most important job is "to connect the people to their purpose."

At USAA, he explained, every employee underwent an immersive four-day cultural orientation and made a promise to provide extraordinary service to people who had done the same for their country—members of the military and their families. That training was no small investment, since the company had more than 20,000 employees. Its lessons were continually reinforced through town hall meetings and other forums where people at all levels asked questions and shared ideas about how to fulfill their purpose.

Before the recession, Anderson would have rejected Robles's statement about purpose as empty, simplistic rhetoric. But having run into a dead end in figuring out how to make his own organization thrive, Anderson was reexamining some of his basic assumptions about management, and he was open to what Robles was saying.

When Anderson returned to DTE's Detroit headquarters, he made a video that articulated his employees' higher purpose. (He got that idea from Robles, too.) It showed DTE's truck drivers, plant operators, corporate leaders, and many others on the job and described the impact of their work on the well-being of the community—the factory workers, teachers, and doctors who needed the energy DTE generated. The first group of professional employees to see the video gave it a standing ovation. When union members viewed it, some were moved to tears. Never before had their work been framed as a meaningful contribution to the greater good. The video brought to life DTE's new statement of purpose: "We serve with our energy, the lifeblood of communities and the engine of progress."

What happened next was even more important: The company's leaders dedicated themselves to supporting that purpose and wove

Idea in Brief

The Problem

You've surely seen this happen more than once: Employees get stuck in a rut, disengage from their work, and stop performing to their potential. So managers respond with tighter oversight and control, yet nothing improves.

The Reason

Most management practices and incentives are based on conventional economic logic, which assumes that employees are self-interested agents. And that assumption becomes a self-fulfilling prophecy.

The Solution

By connecting people with a sense of higher purpose, leaders can inspire them to bring more energy and creativity to their jobs. When employees feel that their work has meaning, they become more committed and engaged. They take risks, learn, and raise their game.

it into onboarding and training programs, corporate meetings, and culture-building activities such as film festivals and sing-alongs. As people judged the purpose to be authentic, a transformation began to take place. Engagement scores climbed. The company received a Gallup Great Workplace Award for five years in a row. And financial performance responded in kind: DTE's stock price more than tripled from the end of 2008 to the end of 2017.

Why did purpose work so well after other interventions had failed? Anderson had previously tried to shake things up by providing training, altering incentives, and increasing managerial oversight, with disappointing results. It turned out that his approach was to blame—not his people.

That's a hard truth to recognize. If, like many executives, you're applying conventional economic logic, you view your employees as self-interested agents and design your organizational practices and culture accordingly, and that hasn't paid off as you'd hoped.

So you now face a choice: You can double down on that approach, on the assumption that you just need more or stricter controls to achieve the desired impact. Or you can align the organization with an authentic higher purpose that intersects with your business interests and helps guide your decisions. If you succeed in doing the latter, your people will try new things, move into deep learning, take risks, and make surprising contributions.

Many executives avoid working on their firms' purpose. Why? Because it defies what they have learned in business school and, perhaps, in subsequent experience: that work is fundamentally contractual, and employees will seek to minimize personal costs and effort.

Those are not necessarily faulty assumptions—indeed, they describe the behavior in many environments reasonably well. However, they also amount to a self-fulfilling prophecy. When managers view employees this way, they create the very problems they expect. Employees choose to respond primarily to the incentives outlined in their contracts and the controls imposed on them. Consequently, they not only fail to see opportunities but also experience conflict, resist feedback, underperform, and personally stagnate. So managers, believing that their assumptions about employees have been validated, exert still more control and rely even more heavily on extrinsic incentives. Employees then narrowly focus on achieving those rewards, typically at the expense of activities that are hard to measure and often ignored, such as mentoring subordinates and sharing best practices. Overarching values and goals become empty words. People do only what they have to do. Results again fall short of expectations, and managers clamp down further.

In this article we provide a framework that can help managers break out of this vicious cycle. In our consulting work with hundreds of organizations and in our research—which includes extensive interviews with dozens of leaders and the development of a theoretical model—we have come to see that when an authentic purpose permeates business strategy and decision making, the personal good and the collective good become one. Positive peer pressure kicks in, and employees are reenergized. Collaboration increases, learning accelerates, and performance climbs. We'll look at how you can set off a similar chain of events in your organization, drawing on examples from a range of companies.

How to Do It

When organizations embrace purpose, it's often because a crisis forces leaders to challenge their assumptions about motivation and performance and to experiment with new approaches. But you don't need to wait for a dire situation. The framework we've developed can help you build a purpose-driven organization when you're *not* backed into a corner. It enables you to overcome the largest barrier to embracing purpose—the cynical "transactional" view of employee motivation—by following eight essential steps.

1. Envision an inspired workforce

According to economists, every employer faces the "principal-agent problem," which is the standard economic model for describing an organization's relationships with its workers. Here's the basic idea: The principal (the employer) and the agent (the employee) form a work contract. The agent is effort-averse. For a certain amount of money, he or she will deliver a certain amount of labor, and no more. Since effort is personally costly, the agent underperforms in providing it unless the principal puts contractual incentives and control systems in place to counter that tendency.

This model precludes the notion of a fully engaged workforce. According to its logic, what Anderson saw at USAA is not possible; it would be foolish to aspire to such an outcome.

One way to change that perception is to expose leaders to positive exceptions to the rule. Consider this July 2015 blog post by Mike Rowe, host of the Discovery Channel show *Dirty Jobs,* about an experience he had at a Hampton Inn:

> I left my hotel room this morning to jump out of a perfectly good airplane, and saw part of a man standing in the hallway. His feet were on a ladder. The rest of him was somewhere in the ceiling.
>
> I introduced myself, and asked what he was doing. Along with satisfying my natural curiosity, it seemed a good way to delay my appointment with gravity, which I was in no hurry to keep. His name is Corey Mundle. . . . We quickly got to talking.

"Well, Mike, here's the problem," he said. "My pipe has a crack in it, and now my hot water is leaking into my laundry room. I've got to turn off my water, replace my old pipe, and get my new one installed before my customers notice there's a problem."

I asked if he needed a hand, and he told me the job wasn't dirty enough. We laughed, and Corey asked if he could have a quick photo. I said sure, assuming he'd return the favor. He asked why I wanted a photo of him, and I said it was because I liked his choice of pronouns.

"I like the way you talk about your work," I said. "It's not 'the' hot water, it's 'MY' hot water. It's not 'the' laundry room, it's 'MY' laundry room. It's not 'a' new pipe, it's 'MY' new pipe. Most people don't talk like that about their work. Most people don't own it."

Corey shrugged and said, "This is not 'a' job; this is 'MY' job. I'm glad to have it, and I take pride in everything I do."

He didn't know it, but Corey's words made my job a little easier that day. Because three hours later, when I was trying to work up the courage to leap out of a perfectly good airplane, I wasn't thinking about pulling the ripcord on the parachute— I was thinking about pulling MY ripcord. On MY parachute.

Corey Mundle is a purpose-driven employee. Instead of minimizing effort as a typical "agent" would, he takes ownership. The fact that people like him exist is important. When coaching executives on how to do purpose work in their organizations, we often tell them, "If it is real, it is possible." If you can find one positive example—a person, a team, a unit that exceeds the norms—you can inspire others. Look for excellence, examine the purpose that drives the excellence, and then imagine it imbuing your entire workforce.

2. Discover the purpose

At a global oil company, we once met with members of a task force asked by the CEO to work on defining the organization's purpose. They handed us a document representing months of work; it articulated a purpose, a mission, and a set of values. We told them it had no power—their analysis and debate had produced only platitudes.

The members of the task force had used only their heads to invent a higher purpose intended to capture employees' hearts. But you do not invent a higher purpose; it already exists. You can discover it through empathy—by feeling and understanding the deepest common needs of your workforce. That involves asking provocative questions, listening, and reflecting.

Deborah Ball, a former dean of the School of Education at the University of Michigan, provides a good example. Like most companies, professional schools experience "mission drift." As a new dean, Ball wanted to clarify her organization's purpose so that she could increase employees' focus, commitment, and collaboration.

To "learn and unlearn the organization," as she put it, she interviewed every faculty member. She expected to find much diversity of opinion—and she did. But she also found surprising commonality, what she called "an emerging story" about the faculty's strong desire to have a positive impact on society. Ball wrote up what she heard and shared it with the people she interviewed. She listened to their reactions and continued to refine their story.

This was not just a listening tour. It was an extended, disciplined, iterative process. Ball says, "You identify gold nuggets, work with them, clarify them, integrate them, and continually feed them back." She refers to the process as "collective creation," borrowing a phrase from agile and design-thinking methodologies.

As that work continued, it became clear that the school had strengths it could use for social good. For example, it had the capacity to influence how other institutions around the world trained teachers, addressed issues of educational affordability, and served underrepresented populations. Ball concluded that these foci had the greatest potential to integrate faculty members' efforts, draw impressive new hires, and attract funding for research. So she highlighted them as crucial elements of the school's collective identity.

3. Recognize the need for authenticity

Purpose has become a popular topic. Even leaders who don't believe in it face pressure from board members, investors, employees, and other stakeholders to articulate a higher purpose. This sometimes leads to statements like the one produced by the task force at the oil company. When a company announces its purpose and values but the words don't govern the behavior of senior leadership, they ring hollow. Everyone recognizes the hypocrisy, and employees become more cynical. The process does harm.

Some CEOs intuitively understand this danger. One actually told his senior leadership team that he didn't want to do purpose work, because organizations are political systems and hypocrisy is inevitable. His statement illustrates an important point: The assumption that people act only out of self-interest also gets applied to leaders, who are often seen as disingenuous if they claim other motivations.

A member of the team responded, "Why don't we change that? Let's identify a purpose and a set of values, and live them with integrity." That earnest comment punctured the existing skepticism, and the team moved ahead.

For an illustration of a purpose that does shape behavior, let's look at Sandler O'Neill and Partners, a midsize investment bank that helps financial institutions raise capital. The company was successful in its niche and focused on the usual goal of maximizing shareholder value. However, on September 11, 2001, disaster struck. Located in the Twin Towers in New York, the company felt the full brunt of the terrorist attack. Jimmy Dunne, soon to lead the firm's executive team, learned that over one-third of Sandler's people, including its top two executives, were dead, and the company's physical infrastructure was devastated. Many of its computers and customer records were gone.

As the crisis unfolded, despite the exceptionally heavy demands of attending to business, Dunne made the decision that a Sandler partner would attend the funeral of every fallen employee, which meant that he attended many funerals. As a result of witnessing so much suffering, he began to realize that the purpose of his firm was not only to satisfy customers and create shareholder value but also to treat employees like valued human beings.

That led to some sharp departures from protocol. For example, he asked his CFO to pay the families of all the dead employees their salaries and bonuses through December 31, 2001—and then asked if the company could do the same for all of 2002. The CFO said the firm could survive, but doing this would be inconsistent with its fiduciary responsibility to the partners. So the firm offered to buy out the ownership stake of any partner at par. Not one accepted.

If your purpose is authentic, people know, because it drives every decision and you do things other companies would not, like paying the families of dead employees. Dunne told us that often an organization discovers its purpose and values when things are going badly—and that its true nature is revealed by what its leaders do in difficult times. He said, "You judge people not by how much they give but by how much they have left after they give."

4. Turn the authentic message into a constant message

When we spoke with the CEO of a global professional services company about how to build a purpose-driven organization, his first question was "When will I be done?"

We responded by telling a story about another CEO, who had been trying to transform his construction company for a year. He showed us his plan and asked our opinion. We told him he deserved an A–. Why wasn't it an A? After giving speeches for a year, he thought he was finished—but his people were just beginning to hear his message. He needed to keep clarifying the organization's purpose for as long as he was CEO. When we told him that, he sank into his chair.

In contrast, Tony Meola, the recently retired head of U.S. consumer operations at Bank of America, is a leader who understands the ongoing nature of purpose work. He says one thing that makes it relentlessly difficult is that it involves getting institutions to shift direction—and existing cultures tend to impede movement. As extensions of the culture, managers, too, end up resisting the change. Other impediments are organizational complexity and competing demands.

Meola overcame those obstacles by clarifying the purpose of his division: treating operational excellence as a destination and allowing no other pressures to distract from it. He emphasized operational skills and leadership in employee training and development, and he brought that focus to every conversation, every decision, every problem his team faced, always asking, "Will this make us better operators?" He says, "When you hold it constant like that, when you never waver, an amazing thing happens. The purpose sinks into the collective conscience. The culture changes, and the organization begins to perform at a higher level. Processes become simpler and easier to execute and sustain. People start looking for permanent solutions rather than stop-gap measures that create more inefficiencies through process variations."

Embracing this mindset meant saying no to anything that didn't reflect it. In the division's call center, for example, there had been a proposal to invest additional resources in technology and people so that the group could solve customers' problems faster and better. But the project was rejected because when managers and employees used their stated purpose as a filter and asked themselves whether that investment would make them better operators, the answer was no. What the company really needed to do, they determined, was examine how the operations themselves could be improved to eliminate failures that produced call center inquiries in the first place.

When a leader communicates the purpose with authenticity and constancy, as Meola did, employees recognize his or her commitment, begin to believe in the purpose themselves, and reorient. The change is signaled from the top, and then it unfolds from the bottom.

5. Stimulate individual learning
Conventional economic logic tends to rely on external motivators. As leaders embrace higher purpose, however, they recognize that learning and development are powerful incentives. Employees actually want to think, learn, and grow.

At the St. Louis–based not-for-profit The Mission Continues, whose purpose is to rehabilitate and reintegrate into society wounded and disabled war veterans, new hires are assigned a large amount of work. The underlying philosophy is that when a leader gives someone a difficult challenge, it shows faith in that person's potential. The job becomes an incubator for learning and development, and along the way the employee gains confidence and becomes more committed to the organization and the higher purpose that drives it.

By helping employees understand the relationship between the higher purpose and the learning process, leaders can strengthen it. People at The Mission Continues are required to reflect on that relationship often. Every two weeks they produce a written document describing their purpose, their strengths, and their development. The exercise is not repetitive, because the experiences change, as do the lessons learned. This practice is consistent with research on effective leadership development approaches. In modern organizations, new experiences tend to come easily, but reflection does not.

At The Mission Continues, the employees have become adaptive and proactive. There is less need for managerial control, because they know the purpose and see how it has changed them for the better. You can liken this clear sense of direction to "commander's intent" in the military. If soldiers know and internalize a commander's strategic purpose, they can carry out the mission even when the commander isn't there. This means, of course, that the leader must communicate the organization's higher purpose with utter clarity so that employees can make use of their local information and take initiative. Research by business school professors Claudine Gartenberg, Andrea Prat, and George Serafeim shows how critical this is in corporations, too—it is not unique to nonprofits.

6. Turn midlevel managers into purpose-driven leaders

To build an inspired, committed workforce, you'll need middle managers who not only know the organization's purpose but also deeply connect with it and lead with moral power. That goes way beyond what most companies ask of their midlevel people.

Consider KPMG, a Big Four accounting cooperative with thousands of partners. For decades those partners approached leadership like accounting. They were careful in their observations, exact in their assessments, and cautious about their decisions, because that was the cultural tone set at the top. Senior leaders were not inclined to get emotional about ideals, and neither were the partners. As a result, employees at all levels tended to make only safe, incremental improvements.

But then KPMG went through a transformation. The company began to explore the notion of purpose. Searching its history, its leaders were surprised to find that it had made many significant contributions to major world events. After conducting and analyzing hundreds of employee interviews, they concluded that KPMG's purpose was to help clients "inspire confidence and empower change."

These five words evoked a sense of awe in the firm, but KPMG's top executives avoided the temptation to turn them into a marketing slogan. Instead, they set out to connect every leader and manager to the purpose. They began by talking openly about their own sense of purpose and meaning. When this had an impact, they recognized that the partners needed to do the same with their teams. When senior management shared these expectations, the partners were open to them but did not feel equipped to meet them. So the accounting firm invested in a new kind of training, in which the partners learned how to tell compelling stories that conveyed their sense of personal identity and professional purpose.

Though applying that training was difficult—it was a real stretch for experts in investment, real estate, tax, risk consulting, and so on—the culture did change. Today the partners communicate their personal purpose to their teams and discuss how it links to their professional lives and the organization's reason for being. In doing so, they are modeling a vulnerability and authenticity that no one had previously expected to see at the middle levels of this accounting firm.

7. Connect the people to the purpose

Once leaders at the top and in the middle have internalized the organization's purpose, they must help frontline employees see how it connects with their day-to-day tasks. But a top-down mandate does not work. Employees need to help drive this process, because then the purpose is more likely to permeate the culture, shaping behavior even when managers aren't right there to watch how people are handling things. Our best illustration again comes from KPMG, where employees were encouraged to share their own accounts of how they were making a difference. This evolved into a remarkable program called the 10,000 Stories Challenge. It gave employees access to a user-friendly design program and invited them to create posters that would answer the question "What do you do at KPMG?" while capturing their passion and connecting it to the organization's purpose.

Each participating employee created a purpose-driven headline, such as "I Combat Terrorism," and under it wrote a clarifying statement, such as "KPMG helps scores of financial institutions prevent money laundering, keeping financial resources out of the hands of terrorists and criminals." Beneath the statement, the employee would insert his or her picture. Each poster carried the tagline "Inspire Confidence. Empower Change."

In June company leaders announced that if the staff could create 10,000 posters by Thanksgiving, two extra days would be added to the holiday break. Employees hit that benchmark within a month. But then the process went viral—after the reward had already been earned. Twenty-seven thousand people produced 42,000 posters (some individuals made multiple submissions, and teams produced them as well). KPMG had found a brilliant way to help employees personally identify with its collective purpose.

Once the firm's overall transformation had taken root, surveys showed that employees' pride in their work had increased, and engagement scores reached record levels. The firm eventually climbed 31 places, to the number 12 spot, on *Fortune*'s 100 Best Companies to Work For list, making it the highest ranked of the Big Four. Recruiting improved, and as turnover decreased, costs dropped.

8. Unleash the positive energizers

Every organization has a pool of change agents that usually goes untapped. We refer to this pool as the network of positive energizers. Spread randomly throughout the organization are mature, purpose-driven people with an optimistic orientation, people like Corey Mundle at Hampton Inn. They naturally inspire others. They're open and willing to take initiative. Once enlisted, they can assist with every step of the cultural change. These people are easy to identify, and others trust them.

We have helped launch such networks in numerous organizations, including Prudential Retirement, Kelly Services, and DTE

Energy. Typically, at an initial meeting, senior leaders invite network members to become involved in the design and execution of the change process. Within minutes, there is buy-in. Regular meetings are scheduled. The energizers go out, share ideas, and return with feedback and new ideas. They're willing to tell the truth and openly challenge assumptions.

There is often another benefit, as the experience of one human resources director illustrates. After establishing a network of positive energizers in a major professional services firm, she called us to report that she felt overwhelmed—in a good way—by the interest and commitment of the people she had assembled. They were an amazing resource that, until now, had gone completely unrecognized. They cared as deeply as she did about the organization's purpose and getting colleagues to embrace it. She said, "I no longer feel alone."

Although a higher purpose does not guarantee economic benefits, we have seen impressive results in many organizations. And other research—particularly the Gartenberg study, which included 500,000 people across 429 firms and involved 917 firm-year observations from 2006 to 2011—suggests a positive impact on both operating financial performance (return on assets) and forward-looking measures of performance (Tobin's Q and stock returns) when the purpose is communicated with clarity.

So purpose is not just a lofty ideal; it has practical implications for your company's financial health and competitiveness. People who find meaning in their work don't hoard their energy and dedication. They give them freely, defying conventional economic assumptions about self-interest. They grow rather than stagnate. They do more—and they do it better.

By tapping into that power, you can transform an entire organization.

Originally published in July–August 2018. **Reprint** R1804E

Creating the Best Workplace on Earth

by Rob Goffee and Gareth Jones

SUPPOSE YOU WANT TO DESIGN the best company on earth to work for. What would it be like? For three years we've been investigating this question by asking hundreds of executives in surveys and in seminars all over the world to describe their ideal organization. This mission arose from our research into the relationship between authenticity and effective leadership. Simply put, people will not follow a leader they feel is inauthentic. But the executives we questioned made it clear that to be authentic, they needed to work for an authentic organization.

What did they mean? Many of their answers were highly specific, of course. But underlying the differences of circumstance, industry, and individual ambition we found six common imperatives. Together they describe an organization that operates at its fullest potential by allowing people to do their best work.

We call this "the organization of your dreams." In a nutshell, it's a company where individual differences are nurtured; information is not suppressed or spun; the company adds value to employees, rather than merely extracting it from them; the organization stands for something meaningful; the work itself is intrinsically rewarding; and there are no stupid rules.

These principles might all sound commonsensical. Who wouldn't want to work in a place that follows them? Executives are certainly aware of the benefits, which many studies have confirmed. Take these two examples: Research from the Hay Group finds that highly engaged employees are, on average, 50% more likely to exceed expectations than the least-engaged workers. And companies with highly engaged people outperform firms with the most disengaged folks—by 54% in employee retention, by 89% in customer satisfaction, and by fourfold in revenue growth. Recent research by our London Business School colleague Dan Cable shows that employees who feel welcome to express their authentic selves at work exhibit higher levels of organizational commitment, individual performance, and propensity to help others.

Yet, few, if any, organizations possess all six virtues. Several of the attributes run counter to traditional practices and ingrained habits. Others are, frankly, complicated and can be costly to implement. Some conflict with one another. Almost all require leaders to carefully balance competing interests and to rethink how they allocate their time and attention.

So the company of your dreams remains largely aspirational. We offer our findings, therefore, as a challenge: an agenda for leaders and organizations that aim to create the most productive and rewarding working environment possible.

Let People Be Themselves

When companies try to accommodate differences, they too often confine themselves to traditional diversity categories—gender, race, age, ethnicity, and the like. These efforts are laudable, but the executives we interviewed were after something more subtle—differences in perspectives, habits of mind, and core assumptions.

The vice chancellor at one of the world's leading universities, for instance, would walk around campus late at night to locate the research hot spots. A tough-minded physicist, he expected to find them in the science labs. But much to his surprise, he discovered them in all kinds of academic disciplines—ancient history, drama, the Spanish department.

Idea in Brief

You want to design the best company on earth to work for. What would it be like? The response from hundreds of executives all over the world, in a nutshell, is that their dream organization is a place where:

- You can be yourself.
- You're told what's really going on.
- Your strengths are magnified.
- The company stands for something meaningful.
- Your daily work is rewarding.
- Stupid rules don't exist.

Those virtues seem like common sense, but few companies exemplify all six. Some of the attributes conflict, and many are complicated, costly, or time-consuming to implement. Almost all of them require leaders to carefully balance competing interests and reallocate their time and attention. So the list stands as a challenge: It's an agenda for executives who aim to create the most productive and rewarding working environment possible.

The ideal organization is aware of dominant currents in its culture, work habits, dress code, traditions, and governing assumptions but, like the chancellor, makes explicit efforts to transcend them. We are talking not just about the buttoned-down financial services company that embraces the IT guys in shorts and sandals, but also the hipster organization that doesn't look askance when someone wears a suit. Or the place where nearly everyone comes in at odd hours but that accommodates the one or two people who prefer a 9-to-5 schedule.

For example, at LVMH, the world's largest luxury-goods company (and growing rapidly), you'd expect to find brilliant, creative innovators like Marc Jacobs and Phoebe Philo. And you do. But alongside them you also encounter a higher-than-expected proportion of executives and specialists who monitor and assess ideas with an analytical business focus. One of the ingredients in LVMH's success is having a culture where opposite types can thrive and work cooperatively. Careful selection is part of the secret: LVMH looks for creative people who want their designs to be marketable and who, in turn, are more likely to appreciate monitors who are skilled at spotting commercial potential.

The benefits of tapping the full range of people's knowledge and talents may be obvious, yet it's not surprising that so few companies do it. For one thing, uncovering biases isn't easy. (Consider the assumption the diligent chancellor made when he equated research intensity with late-night lab work.) More fundamentally, though, efforts to nurture individuality run up against countervailing efforts to increase organizational effectiveness by forging clear incentive systems and career paths. Competence models, appraisal systems, management by objectives, and tightly defined recruitment policies all narrow the range of acceptable behavior.

Companies that succeed in nurturing individuality, therefore, may have to forgo some degree of organizational orderliness. Take Arup, perhaps the world's most creative engineering and design company. Many iconic buildings bear the mark of Arup's distinctive imprint—from the Sydney Opera House to the Centre Pompidou to the Beijing Water Cube.

Arup approaches its work holistically. When the firm builds a suspension bridge, for example, it looks beyond the concerns of the immediate client to the region that relies on the bridge. To do so, Arup's people collaborate with mathematicians, economists, artists, and politicians alike. Accordingly, Arup considers the capacity to absorb different skill sets and personalities as key to its strategy. "We want there to be interesting parts that don't quite fit in . . . that take us places where we didn't expect to get to," says chairman Philip Dilley. "That's part of my job now—to prevent it from becoming totally orderly."

Conventional appraisal systems don't work in such a world, so Arup doesn't use quantitative performance-measurement systems or articulate a corporate policy on how employees should progress. Managers make their expectations clear, but individuals decide how to meet them. "Self-determination means setting your own path and being accountable for your success," a senior HR official explains. "Development and progression is your own business, with our support."

If this sounds too chaotic for a more conventional company, consider Waitrose, one of Britain's most successful food retailers, according to measures as diverse as market share, profitability, and customer and staff loyalty. In an industry that necessarily focuses on executing processes efficiently, Waitrose sees its competitive edge in nurturing the small sparks of creativity that make a big difference to the customer experience.

Waitrose is a cooperative: Every employee is a co-owner who shares in the company's annual profits. So the source of staff loyalty is not much of a mystery. But even so, the company goes to great lengths to draw out and support people's personal interests. If you want to learn piano, Waitrose will pay half the cost of the lessons. There's a thriving club culture—cooking, crafts, swimming, and so on. We have a friend whose father learned to sail because he worked for this organization. In that way, Waitrose strives to create an atmosphere where people feel comfortable being themselves. We were struck when a senior executive told us, "Friends and family would recognize me at work."

"Great retail businesses depend on characters who do things a bit differently," another executive explained. "Over the years we have had lots of them. We must be careful to cherish them and make sure our systems don't squeeze them out."

Pursuit of predictability leads to a culture of conformity, what Emile Durkheim called "mechanical solidarity." But companies like LVMH, Arup, and Waitrose are forged out of "organic solidarity"— which, Durkheim argued, rests on the productive exploitation of differences. Why go to all the trouble? We think Ted Mathas, head of the mutual insurance company New York Life, explains it best: "When I was appointed CEO, my biggest concern was, would this [job] allow me to truly say what I think? I needed to be myself to do a good job. Everybody does."

Unleash the Flow of Information

The organization of your dreams does not deceive, stonewall, distort, or spin. It recognizes that in the age of Facebook, WikiLeaks, and Twitter, you're better off telling people the truth before someone else does. It respects its employees' need to know what's really going on

The "Dream Company" Diagnostic

HOW CLOSE IS YOUR ORGANIZATION to the ideal? To find out, check off each statement that applies. The more checkmarks you have, the closer you are to the dream.

Let Me Be Myself

- ☐ I'm the same person at home as I am at work.
- ☐ I feel comfortable being myself.
- ☐ We're all encouraged to express our differences.
- ☐ People who think differently from most do well here.
- ☐ Passion is encouraged, even when it leads to conflict.
- ☐ More than one type of person fits in here.

Tell Me What's Really Going On

- ☐ We're all told the whole story.
- ☐ Information is not spun.
- ☐ It's not disloyal to say something negative.
- ☐ My manager wants to hear bad news.
- ☐ Top executives want to hear bad news.
- ☐ Many channels of communication are available to us.
- ☐ I feel comfortable signing my name to comments I make.

Discover and Magnify My Strengths

- ☐ I am given the chance to develop.
- ☐ Every employee is given the chance to develop.
- ☐ The best people want to strut their stuff here.
- ☐ The weakest performers can see a path to improvement.
- ☐ Compensation is fairly distributed throughout the organization.

---

so that they can do their jobs, particularly in volatile environments where it's already difficult to keep everyone aligned and where workers at all levels are being asked to think more strategically. You'd imagine that would be self-evident to managers everywhere. In reality, the

☐ We generate value for ourselves by adding value to others.

Make Me Proud I Work Here

☐ I know what we stand for.

☐ I value what we stand for.

☐ I want to exceed my current duties.

☐ Profit is not our overriding goal.

☐ I am accomplishing something worthwhile.

☐ I like to tell people where I work.

Make My Work Meaningful

☐ My job is meaningful to me.

☐ My duties make sense to me.

☐ My work gives me energy and pleasure.

☐ I understand how my job fits with everyone else's.

☐ Everyone's job is necessary.

☐ At work we share a common cause.

Don't Hinder Me with Stupid Rules

☐ We keep things simple.

☐ The rules are clear and apply equally to everyone.

☐ I know what the rules are for.

☐ Everyone knows what the rules are for.

☐ We, as an organization, resist red tape.

☐ Authority is respected.

barriers to what we call "radical honesty"—that is, entirely candid, complete, clear, and timely communication—are legion.

Some managers see parceling out information on a need-to-know basis as important to maintaining efficiency. Others practice a seemingly benign type of paternalism, reluctant to worry staff with certain information or to identify a problem before having a solution. Some feel an obligation to put a positive spin on even the most negative situations out of a best-foot-forward sense of loyalty to the organization.

The reluctance to be the bearer of bad news is deeply human, and many top executives well know that this tendency can strangle the flow of critical information. Take Novo Nordisk's Mads Øvlisen, who was CEO in the 1990s, when violations of FDA regulations at the company's Danish insulin-production facilities became so serious that U.S. regulators nearly banned the insulin from the U.S. market. Incredible as it seems in hindsight, no one told Øvlisen about the situation. That's because Novo Nordisk operated under a culture in which the executive management board was never supposed to receive bad news.

The company took formal steps to rectify the situation, redesigning the company's entire quality-management system—its processes, procedures, and training of all involved personnel. Eventually, those practices were extended to new-product development, manufacturing, distribution, sales, and support systems. More generally, a vision, core values, and a set of management principles were explicitly articulated as the Novo Nordisk Way. To get at the root cause of the crisis, Øvlisen also set out to create a new culture of honesty through a process he called "organizational facilitation"—that is, facilitation of the flow of honest information.

A core team of facilitators (internal management auditors) with long organizational experience now regularly visit all of the company's worldwide affiliates. They interview randomly selected employees and managers to assess whether the Novo Nordisk Way is being practiced. Employees know, for instance, that they must inform all stakeholders both within and outside the organization of what's happening, even when something goes wrong, as quickly as possible. Does this really happen? Many employees have told us that they appreciate these site visits because they foster honest conversations about fundamental business values and processes.

Radical honesty is not easy to implement. It requires opening many different communication channels, which can be time-consuming to maintain. And for previously insulated top managers, it can be somewhat ego-bruising. Witness what ensued when Novo Nordisk recently banned soda from all its buildings. PeopleCom, the company's internal news site, was flooded with hundreds of passionate responses. Some people saw it as an attack on personal freedom. ("I wonder what will be the next thing NN will 'help' me not to do," wrote one exasperated employee. "Ban fresh fruit in an effort to reduce sugar consumption?") Others defended the policy as a logical extension of the company's focus on diabetes. ("We can still purchase our own sugary soft drinks . . . Novo Nordisk shouldn't be a 7-Eleven.") That all these comments were signed indicates how much honesty has infused Novo Nordisk's culture.

Trade secrets will always require confidentiality. And we don't want to suggest that honesty will necessarily stop problems from arising, particularly in highly regulated industries that routinely find themselves under scrutiny. We maintain, though, that executives should err on the side of transparency far more than their instincts suggest. Particularly today, when trust levels among both employees and customers are so low and background noise is so high, organizations must work very hard to communicate what's going on if they are to be heard and believed.

Magnify People's Strengths

The ideal company makes its best employees even better—and the least of them better than they ever thought they could be. In robust economies, when competition for talent is fierce, it's easy to see that the benefits of developing existing staff outweigh the costs of finding new workers. But even then, companies grumble about losing their investment when people decamp for more-promising opportunities. In both good times and bad, managers are far more often rewarded for minimizing labor costs than for the longer-term goal of increasing workers' effectiveness. Perhaps that explains why this aspiration, while so widely recognized and well understood, often remains unfulfilled.

Elite universities and hospitals, Goldman Sachs and McKinsey, and design firms like Arup have all been adding value to valuable people for a very long time. Google and Apple are more recent examples. They do this in myriad ways—by providing networks, creative interaction with peers, stretch assignments, training, and a brand that confers elite status on employees. None of this is rocket science, nor is it likely to be news to anyone.

But the challenge of finding, training, and retaining excellent workers is not confined to specialized, high-tech, or high-finance industries. We contend that the employee-employer relationship is shifting in many industries from how much value can be extracted from workers to how much can be instilled in them. At heart, that's what productivity improvement really means.

Take McDonald's, a company founded on the primacy of cost efficiency. In an economy with plenty of people looking for jobs, McDonald's nevertheless focuses on the growth paths of its frontline workers—and on a large scale. In the UK, the company invests £36 million ($55 million) a year in giving its 87,500 employees the chance to gain a wide range of nationally recognized academic qualifications while they work. One of the largest apprenticeship providers in the country, McDonald's has awarded more than 35,000 such qualifications to employees since the program's launch in 2006. Every week the equivalent of six full classes of students acquire formal credentials in math and English. Every day another 20 employees earn an apprenticeship qualification.

Like many large companies, McDonald's has extensive management training programs for its executives, but the firm also extends that effort to restaurant general managers, department managers, and shift managers who, as the day-to-day leaders on the front lines, are taught the communication and coaching skills they need to motivate crews and to hit their shifts' sales targets. The return on the company's investment is measured not in terms of increased revenue or profitability but in lower turnover of hourly managers and their crews. Turnover has declined steadily since the programs were initiated, as reflected in the Great Place to Work Institute's recognition of McDonald's as one of the 50 best workplaces every year since 2007.

To get a sense of how far employee development can be taken, consider Games Makers, the volunteer training effort mounted by the London Organising Committee of the Olympic Games. LOCOG was responsible for the largest peacetime workforce ever assembled in the UK. It coordinated the activities of more than 100,000 subcontractors, 70,000 Games Makers volunteers, and 8,000 paid staff. Games Makers used bold, imaginative schemes to employ people who had never worked or volunteered before. Through its Trailblazer program, for example, paid staff learned how to work effectively with volunteers of all social backgrounds. Through a partnership with other state agencies, the Personal Best program enabled more than 7,500 disadvantaged, long-term-unemployed individuals, some with physical or learning disabilities, to earn a job qualification. Games Makers' School Leavers program targeted students who have left school in east London, the host borough for the games, by granting them two three-month placements that, upon successful completion, were followed by a contract for employment until the end of the event. LOCOG's model has inspired government agencies and private-sector employment bureaus in the UK to rewrite their work-engagement guidelines to enable them to tap into—and make productive—a far wider range of people than had previously been considered employable.

We recognize that promising to bring out the best in everyone is a high-risk, high-reward strategy. It raises reputational capital, and such capital is easily destroyed. Goldman Sachs, for one, spent years building its reputation as the most exciting investment bank of all. That's why Greg Smith's scathing resignation letter, accusing the company of not living up to its own standards, was so damaging. Once a company heads down this road, it has to keep going.

Stand for More Than Shareholder Value

People want to be a part of something bigger than themselves, something they can believe in. "I've worked in organizations where people try to brainwash me about the virtues of the brand," one seminar participant told us. "I want to work in an organization where I can really feel where the company comes from and what it stands for so that I can live the brand."

It has become commonplace to assert that organizations need shared meaning, and this is surely so. But shared meaning is about more than fulfilling your mission statement—it's about forging and maintaining powerful connections between personal and organizational values. When you do that, you foster individuality and a strong culture at the same time.

Some people might argue that certain companies have an inherent advantage in this area. An academic colleague once asked us if we were working with anyone interesting. When we mentioned Novo Nordisk, he produced from his briefcase a set of Novo pens for injecting insulin and said simply, "They save my life every day." Engineers who design the side bars for BMW's mini have been known to wake up at 4:00 in the morning to write down ideas that will make the cars safer. And that might be expected of people drawn to the idea of building "the ultimate driving machine."

But the advantage these companies have is not the businesses they're in. The connections they forge stem, rather, from the way they do business. To understand how that works more generally, consider Michael Barry, who once was a teacher made redundant by state spending cuts. Three decades later, the experience remained vividly traumatic: "It was a case of 'last in, first out,' nothing to do with merit. I decided I never wanted to lose my job like that again. I researched things quite carefully, looking for places that were clear about what they wanted."

And where did this idealistic man go? He became an insurance salesman for New York Life. "It is a very different company—from the top down," he said, when we asked him what connection he felt to the company. He further explained it this way: "Back when other life insurance companies were demutualizing and becoming financial services supermarkets, New York Life made it very clear that life insurance would remain our core focus. The agents didn't like it [at first]—they felt they were losing the opportunity to make more money. But Sy Sternberg, the CEO at that time, went to public forums with the agents and pulled no punches. He told us, 'We are a life insurance company, and we are good at it.'" This is more than a business strategy, Barry says. "It's how we operate every day. This is not a place where we wriggle out of claims. One man took out a life policy, went home to write out the check. It was on his desk when he died that night. The policy was unpaid, but we paid the claim. The agents really buy into this."

Current CEO Ted Mathas acknowledges that New York Life's status as a mutual company gives it an advantage in claiming that profit is not all that matters. But he argues that the same logic applies for public firms—that profit is (or should be) an outcome of the pursuit of other, more meaningful goals. Again, this is hardly a new idea. "But many companies in public ownership have lost their way and with it a sense of who they are," Mathas suggests, and we agree.

Show How the Daily Work Makes Sense

Beyond shared meaning, the executives we've spoken to want something else. They seek to derive meaning from their daily activities.

This aspiration cannot be fulfilled in any comprehensive way through job enrichment add-on. It requires nothing less than a deliberate reconsideration of the tasks each person is performing. Do those duties make sense? Why are they what they are? Are they as engaging as they can be? This is a huge, complex undertaking.

Take John Lewis, the parent company of Waitrose and the department store Peter Jones. In 2012 it completed a review of its more than 2,200 jobs, slotting them within a hierarchy of 10 levels, to make it easier for employees to take advantage of opportunities across the organization. This sounds like a homogenizing move, and it might be at a traditional company. But at John Lewis, which operates for the benefit of its employee owners, it was a deliberate effort to match its people with the work they want to do.

Or consider Rabobank Nederland, the banking arm of the largest financial services provider in the Netherlands, Rabobank Group. After several years of development, the bank has rolled out Rabo Unplugged, an organizational and technical infrastructure that allows employees to connect to one another from practically anywhere while still meeting the stringent encryption standards that banking systems require. With no fixed offices or rigid job descriptions, Rabobank's employees are, like Arup's, responsible for the results of their work. But they are free to choose how, where, when, and with whom to carry it out. This approach requires managers to place an extraordinary amount of trust in subordinates, and it demands that employees become more entrepreneurial and collaborative.

Beyond reconsidering individual roles, making work rewarding may mean rethinking the way companies are led. Arup's organization, which might be described as "extreme seamless," is one possible model. As such, it takes some getting used to. In describing how this works in Arup's Associates unit, board member Tristram Carfrae explains: "We have architects, engineers, quantity surveyors, and project managers in the same room together . . . people who genuinely want to submerge their own egos into the collective and not [be led] in the classic sense." That was a challenge for Carfrae, who as a structural engineer wrestled with the question of when to impose his will on the team and push it toward a structural, rather than a mechanical or an architecturally oriented, solution. To participate in such an evenhanded, interdependent environment is extremely hard, he says. There were "incredible rewards when it worked well and incredible frustrations when it didn't."

We don't wish to underplay this challenge. But we suggest that the benefits of rising to it are potentially very great. Where work is meaningful, it typically becomes a cause, as it is for the engineers at BMW and the agents at New York Life. We also acknowledge an element of risk: When we interviewed legendary games designer Will Wright, he told us that his primary loyalty was not to his company, Electronic Arts, but to the project—originally for him the record-breaking Sims franchise and, more recently, Spore. Wright ultimately left EA to start his own company, in which EA became a joint investor.

The challenge is similar to that of fostering personal growth. If you don't do it, the best people may leave or never consider you at all. Or your competitors may develop the potential in people you've overlooked. When you do make the investment, your staff members become more valuable to you and your competitors alike. The trick, then, is to make it meaningful for them to stay.

Have Rules People Can Believe In

No one should be surprised that, for many people, the dream organization is free of arbitrary restrictions. But it does not obliterate all rules. Engineers, even at Arup, must follow procedures and tight quality controls—or buildings will collapse.

Organizations need structure. Markets and enterprises need rules. As successful entrepreneurial businesses grow, they often come to believe that new, complicated processes will undermine their culture. But systematization need not lead to bureaucratization, not if people understand what the rules are for and view them as legitimate. Take Vestergaard Frandsen, a start-up social enterprise that makes mosquito netting for the developing world. The company is mastering the art of behavior codes that can help structure its growing operations without jeopardizing its culture. Hiring (and firing) decisions are intentionally simple—only one level of approval is required for each position. Regional directors have significant freedom within clear deadlines and top- and bottom-line targets. Knowledge-management systems are designed to encourage people to call rather than e-mail one another and to explain why someone is being cc'ed on an e-mail message. Vestergaard sees these simple rules as safeguards rather than threats to its founding values.

Despite the flattening of hierarchies, the ensuing breakdown of organizational boundaries, and the unpredictability of careers, institutions remain what Max Weber calls "imperatively coordinated associations," where respect for authority is crucial for building and maintaining structure. However, we know that, increasingly, employees are skeptical of purely hierarchical power—of fancy job titles and traditional sources of legitimacy such as age and seniority. And they are becoming more suspicious of charisma, as many charismatic leaders turn out to have feet of clay.

What workers need is a sense of moral authority, derived not from a focus on the efficiency of means but from the importance of the ends they produce. The organization of your dreams gives you powerful reasons to submit to its necessary structures that support the organization's purpose. In that company, leaders' authority derives from the answer to a question that Steve Varley, managing partner of Ernst & Young UK, put to senior partners in his inaugural address, after he reported record profits and partners' earnings: "Is that all there is?" (In reply, he proposed a radical new direction—a program called "Growing Successfully, Making the Difference"— aimed at achieving both financial growth and social change.) During the past 30 years we have heard the following kinds of conversations at many organizations: "I'll be home late. I'm working on a cure for migraine." "Still at work. The new U2 album comes out tomorrow— it's brilliant." "Very busy on the plan to take insulin into East Africa." We have never heard this: "I'll be home late. I'm increasing shareholder value."

People want to do good work—to feel they matter in an organization that makes a difference. They want to work in a place that magnifies their strengths, not their weaknesses. For that, they need some autonomy and structure, and the organization must be coherent, honest, and open.

But that's tricky because it requires balancing many competing claims. Achieving the full benefit of diversity means trading the comfort of being surrounded by kindred spirits for the hard work of fitting various kinds of people, work habits, and thought traditions into a vibrant culture. Managers must continually work out when to forge ahead and when to take the time to discuss and compromise.

Our aim here is not to critique modern business structures. But it's hard not to notice that many of the organizations we've highlighted are unusual in their ownership arrangements and ambitions. Featured strongly are partnerships, mutual associations, charitable trusts, and social enterprises. Although all share a desire to generate revenue, few are conventional, large-scale capitalist enterprises.

It would be a mistake to suggest that the organizations are all alike, but two commonalities stand out. First, the institutions are all very clear about what they do well: Novo Nordisk transforms the lives of people with diabetes; Arup creates beautiful environments. Second, the organizations are suspicious, in almost a contrarian way, of fads and fashions that sweep the corporate world. Work can be liberating, or it can be alienating, exploitative, controlling, and homogenizing. Despite the changes that new technologies and new generations bring, the underlying forces of shareholder capitalism and unexamined bureaucracy remain powerful. As you strive to create an authentic organization and fully realize human potential at work, do not underestimate the challenge. If you do, such organizations will remain the exception rather than the rule— for most people, a mere dream.

Originally published in May 2013. Reprint R1305H

Cultural Change That Sticks

by Jon R. Katzenbach, Ilona Steffen, and Caroline Kronley

IN THE EARLY 2000s Aetna was struggling mightily on all fronts. While on the surface revenues remained strong, its rapport with customers and physicians was rapidly eroding, and its reputation was being bludgeoned by lawsuits and a national backlash against health maintenance organizations and managed care (which Aetna had championed). To boot, the company was losing roughly $1 million a day, thanks to cumbersome processes and enormous overhead, as well as unwise acquisitions.

Many of the problems Aetna faced were attributed to its culture—especially its reverence for the company's 150-year history. Once openly known among workers as "Mother Aetna," the culture encouraged employees to be steadfast to the point that they'd become risk-averse, tolerant of mediocrity, and suspicious of outsiders. The prevailing executive mindset was "We take care of our people for life, as long as they show up every day and don't cause trouble." Employees were naturally wary of any potential threat to that bargain. When Aetna merged with U.S. Healthcare, a lower-cost health care provider, in 1996, a major culture clash ensued. But instead of adapting to U.S. Healthcare's more-aggressive ways, the conservative Aetna culture only became more intransigent. Aetna's leaders could make little headway against it, and one CEO was forced out after failing to change it.

What Aetna's management didn't recognize was that you can't trade your company's culture in as if it were a used car. For all its benefits and blemishes, it's a legacy that remains uniquely yours. Unfortunately, it can feel like a millstone when a company is trying to push through a significant change—a merger, for instance, or a turnaround. Cultural inclinations are well entrenched, for good or bad. But it's possible to draw on the positive aspects of culture, turning them to your advantage, and offset some of the negative aspects as you go. This approach makes change far easier to implement.

In late 2000, John W. Rowe, MD, became Aetna's fourth CEO in five years. Employees skeptically prepared for yet another exhausting effort to transform the company into an efficient growth engine. This time, however, they were in for a surprise. Rowe didn't walk in with a new strategy and try to force a cultural shift to achieve it. Instead, right from the start, he, along with Ron Williams (who joined Aetna in 2001 and became its president in 2002), took time to visit the troops, understand their perspective, and involve them in the planning. With other members of the senior team, they sought out employees at all levels—those who were well connected, sensitive to the company culture, and widely respected—to get their input on the strategy as well as their views on both the design and execution of intended process changes.

These conversations helped Rowe and his team identify Aetna's biggest problem: A strategy that focused narrowly on managing medical expenses to reduce the cost of claims while alienating the patients and physicians that were key to Aetna's long-term success. At the same time, they surfaced Aetna's significant cultural strengths: a deep-seated concern about patients, providers, and employers; underlying pride in the history and purpose of the company; widespread respect for peers; and a large group of dedicated professionals.

These insights led Rowe to rethink his approach to the company's turnaround. He declared that instead of just cutting costs, the organization would pursue a strategy he called "the New Aetna." It would

Idea in Brief

Many leaders blame their company's culture for thwarting significant change initiatives, such as mergers or turnarounds.

But when they try to solve the problem by changing the culture, their efforts tend to fizzle, fail, or backfire. The consequences can be severe.

What those leaders don't see is that culture is highly ingrained in the ways people work—and that any company culture has assets. The secret is to make the most of its positive elements—to work with and within the culture, rather than fighting against it.

Leaders should take care to honor their culture's strengths, focusing on changing just a few critical behaviors rather than attempting a wholesale transformation. Once they take this view, some leaders even find that their culture has become their primary competitive advantage. These companies align their business priorities with the culture and use it to sharpen their strategic focus, all the while helping the culture evolve so that it becomes an accelerator of change, not an impediment.

build a winning position in health insurance and a strong brand by attracting and serving both patients and health care providers well. That was an appealing proposition but would require significant restructuring; no one's job was guaranteed. In other words, it was the kind of change that Mother Aetna traditionally resisted with every passive-aggressive move she could muster.

But this time, without ever describing their efforts as "cultural change," top management began with a few interventions. These interventions led to small but significant behavioral changes that, in turn, revitalized Aetna's culture while preserving and championing its strengths. For instance, the New Aetna was specifically designed to reinforce employees' commitment to customers—reflected in the firm's history of responding quickly to natural disasters. Rowe also made a point of reinforcing a longtime strength that had eroded—employees' pride in the company. When, in an off-the-cuff response to a question at a town hall meeting, he highlighted pride as a reason employees should get behind change, he received a spontaneous standing ovation.

So while the plan for change challenged long-held assumptions (among other things, it would require the elimination of 5,000 jobs, with more cuts likely to come), it was embraced by employees. They had been heard and appreciated, and they came to accept the New Aetna.

Indeed, during the next few years it became clear, from surveys, conversations, and observation, that a majority of Aetna's employees felt reinvigorated, enthusiastic, and genuinely proud of the company. And Aetna's financial performance reflected that. By the mid-2000s, the company was earning close to $5 million a day. Its operating income recovered from a $300 million loss to a $1.7 billion gain. From May 2001 to January 2006, its stock price rose steadily, from $5.84 (split adjusted) to $48.40 a share.

Aetna's story (which we have drawn from a draft of an unpublished book by Jon Katzenbach and Roger Bolton, a retired Aetna senior executive) isn't unique. We've known for a long time that it takes years to alter how people think, feel, and behave, and even then, the differences may not be meaningful. When that's the case, an organization with an old, powerful culture can devolve into disaster. This has happened at organizations like Washington Mutual, Home Depot (before its recent turnaround), and the U.S. Marine Corps during the Korean and Vietnam wars.

Happily, it's also possible for a culture to move in the right direction, as we saw at Aetna. After all, cultures do evolve over time—sometimes slipping backward, sometimes progressing—and the best you can do is work *with* and *within them,* rather than fight them. In our research we've found that almost every enterprise that has attained peak performance—including the Four Seasons, Apple, Microsoft, and Southwest Airlines—got there by applying five principles. Such companies see culture as a competitive advantage—an accelerator of change, not an impediment.

In this article, we'll walk through the five principles, using examples from our research and client experience. Following them can help an organization achieve higher performance, better customer focus, and a more coherent and ethical stance.

1. Match Strategy and Culture

Too often a company's strategy, imposed from above, is at odds with the ingrained practices and attitudes of its culture. Executives may underestimate how much a strategy's effectiveness depends on cultural alignment. Culture trumps strategy every time.

Some corporate leaders struggle with cultural intransigence for years, without ever fully focusing on the question: *Why* do we want to change our culture? They don't clearly connect their desired culture with their strategy and business objectives. Many times we've walked into organizations that presented us with an entire laundry list of hoped-for cultural traits: collaborative, innovative, a meritocracy, risk taking, focused on quality, and more. The list is too vague and too long to tackle. It sounds great but provides nothing in the way of differentiation.

Contrast such nebulous aspirations with those in an organization in which a few cultural traits truly do match and support the strategy, like the Mayo Clinic. World renowned for its ability to bring together specialists across a range of medical fields to diagnose and effectively treat the most complex diseases, the clinic promotes unusually high levels of collaboration and teamwork, reinforcing those traits through formal and informal mechanisms.

2. Focus on a Few Critical Shifts in Behavior

Studies show that only 10% of people who have had heart bypass surgery or an angioplasty make major modifications to their diets and lifestyles afterward. We don't alter our behavior even in the face of overwhelming evidence that we should. Change is hard. So you need to choose your battles.

Where do you start? First observe the behavior prevalent in your organization now, and imagine how people would act if your company were at its best, especially if their behavior supported your business objectives. Ask the people in your leadership groups, "If we had the kind of culture we aspire to, in pursuit of the strategy we have chosen, what kinds of new behaviors would be common? And what ingrained behaviors would be gone?"

Say your organization is a former utility or government agency interested in becoming a better service business. If it excelled at service, how would people treat customers differently? What kinds of interactions would be visible in any new offices you opened? How would employees propose new ideas or evaluate one another? How would they raise difficult issues or bring potential problems to others' attention? And how would employees react when they actually saw colleagues doing things differently?

When choosing priorities, it often helps to conduct a series of "safe space" discussions with thoughtful people at different levels throughout your company to learn what behaviors are most affected by the current culture—both positively and negatively. This is what Aetna did. It was also the approach taken by a national retailer that was looking to build a culture with a strong customer focus. The retailer's leaders enlisted the help of internal "exemplars"—people who were known for motivating their teams effectively. A group of senior executives interviewed them and isolated a set of crucial motivating behaviors, such as role-modeling good customer service. Store managers received training in the behaviors, which were also translated into specific tactics, such as ways to greet customers entering the store. The stores that have introduced the new behaviors are already beginning to see results, including improved same-store sales in key product areas and fewer customer complaints.

The behaviors you focus on can be small, as long as they are widely recognized and likely to be emulated. Consider the response one company had to the discovery that a major source of employee frustration was its performance-review process. The company used a 360-degree evaluation mechanism, but employees were often unpleasantly surprised by the results. So management introduced a simple behavior: asking people who were providing input whether they had ever given the feedback to the person being reviewed. As a result of this straightforward question, colleagues began to share constructive criticisms with one another more often, resulting in fewer demotivating surprises and a better dialogue about performance.

The Cultural Slide at Arthur Andersen

ONE OF THE BEST-KNOWN, and yet most misunderstood, examples of cultural backsliding took place at the Arthur Andersen accounting firm.

With practices in more than 30 countries, it was once the envy of professional service firms. Then in 2002 indictments during the Enron investigation forced Andersen into bankruptcy. At the time, many believed that a single client relationship had brought the firm down for largely legal or regulatory reasons. In fact, its fall stemmed from a creeping cultural erosion that had begun decades before the Enron debacle.

At least that was the conclusion of analyst and journalist Charles Ellis, who studied the Andersen failure in depth and described it in an unpublished manuscript, *What It Takes*. "Arthur Andersen, once the world's most admired auditing and professional services firm, descended through level after level of self-destructive decline to its ultimate death," he says. Ellis traces the firm's decline to the 1950s, when its leaders shifted their focus from quality and integrity to beating other firms' revenue numbers and market position.

As Andersen expanded around the world, it abandoned practices geared toward professional excellence, such as a rule that all accountants had to spend two years in auditing and the use of a global profit pool that ensured that all partners had a stake in one another's success. Each new measure, while defensible, made it a little easier to compromise the firm's values. The cultural deterioration also made it easier to ignore many warning signs, including the 1973 bankruptcy of Four Seasons Nursing Centers of America, in which the founder pleaded guilty to securities fraud and Andersen, as the auditor, was indicted. By the time Enron became a key client in the late 1990s and insisted on using only individual accountants and auditors who accepted its questionable practices, the accounting firm's professional culture had already declined past the point of no return. A few modest interventions might have preserved the firm's commitment to integrity and avoided a very public and embarrassing demise.

When a few key behaviors are emphasized heavily, employees will often develop additional ways to reinforce them. As GM was emerging from bankruptcy, the company decided to spur innovation by placing a renewed emphasis on risk taking and the open exchange of ideas. After one colleague complimented another on his performance in a meeting, their team lightheartedly began a practice of handing out "gold star" stickers to recognize colleagues exhibiting strong character and candor. The practice soon began to spread.

While the stickers probably would have been received skeptically as a top-down initiative, as an organic peer-to-peer custom they helped reinforce GM's larger cultural evolution.

3. Honor the Strengths of Your Existing Culture

It's tempting to dwell on the negative traits of your culture, but any corporate culture is a product of good intentions that evolved in unexpected ways and will have many strengths. They might include a deep commitment to customer service (which could manifest itself as a reluctance to cut costs) or a predisposition toward innovation (which sometimes leads to "not invented here" syndrome). If you can find ways to demonstrate the relevance of the original values and share stories that illustrate why people believe in them, they can still serve your company well. Acknowledging the existing culture's assets will also make major change feel less like a top-down imposition and more like a shared evolution.

The same surveys of employee behavior, in-depth interviews, and observation that you use to diagnose your culture's weaknesses can also clarify its strengths. Executives at one financial services firm, for example, conducted a survey to test employees' readiness to follow a strategy that involved going head-to-head with a new, aggressive set of competitors. The survey revealed a number of serious cultural challenges, including passive-aggressive behavior, inconclusive decision making, and pervasive organizational silos. But it also showed that staff members were unusually willing to commit time and effort toward the strategy; they really wanted to help. This enormous strength had been largely untapped. That realization helped executives rethink how they communicated the strategy, and more important, how they interacted with employees to support the new behaviors.

Another way to harness the cultural elements you want to support is by acknowledging them. At Aetna a major turning point came during one question-and-answer session, when a longtime employee said, "Dr. Rowe, I really appreciate your taking the time to explain your new strategy. Can you tell me what it means for someone like me?"

Not an easy question. After a thoughtful pause, Rowe replied, "Well, I guess it is all about restoring the Aetna pride." As we noted earlier, he got a spontaneous standing ovation from the hundreds of attendees. Why had that concept hit such a nerve? Aetna had always had a strong record of responding to natural disasters (including the Great Chicago Fire of 1871 and the 1906 San Francisco earthquake). Its employees were also proud of the many famous people—movie stars, astronauts, sports heroes, and other public figures—that the company insured. It was only as a result of a strong managed-care movement that emerged in the 1980s and 1990s that Aetna had gained a reputation as a stingy, recalcitrant company. Employees stopped feeling good about their association with it. "At cocktail parties," said one longtime Aetna staffer, "I really dreaded the question, Who do you work for?" When Rowe and Williams made "restoring the pride" the core of their message, they touched the hearts of many employees and helped them believe Aetna could regain its former glory.

Another strength companies can leverage is the employees who are already aligned with their strategy and desired culture. Most companies, if they look hard enough, will find that they have pockets of activity where people are already exhibiting the new, desired behaviors every day—just as the "exemplar" store managers did at the retailer.

4. Integrate Formal and Informal Interventions

As you promote critical new behaviors, making people aware of how they affect the company's strategic performance, be sure to integrate formal approaches—like new rules, metrics, and incentives—with informal interactions. (For a menu of tools, see the exhibit "Mechanisms for Getting the Most from Your Culture.") Only a few companies understand how to do this well. In our experience, most corporate leaders favor formal, rational moves and neglect the informal, more emotional side of the organization. They adjust reporting lines, decision rights, processes, and IT systems at the outset but overlook informal mechanisms, such as networking, communities of interest, ad hoc conversations, and peer interactions.

Mechanisms for Getting the Most from Your Culture

Formal

- Reporting structures
- Decision rules and rights
- Business processes and policies
- Training, leadership, and organizational development programs
- Performance management
- Compensation and rewards
- Internal communications
- Councils and committees
- Company events

Informal

- Behavior modeling by senior leaders
- Meaningful manager-employee connections
- Internal, cross-organizational networks
- Ad hoc gatherings
- Peer-to-peer interactions and storytelling
- Communities of interest
- Engagement of exemplars and motivational leaders
- Changes to physical plant, resources, and aesthetics

Google is a good example of a company that makes the most of its informal organization. A senior leader we interviewed there compared the company to universities that plan out paved walkways when they expand their campuses. At Google, he said, "we would wait to do the walkways until the employees had worn informal pathways through the grass—and then pave over only those getting the most use."

Whether formal or informal, interventions should do two things: reach people at an emotional level (invoking altruism, pride, and how they feel about the work itself) and tap rational self-interest (providing money, position, and external recognition to those who come on board).

At Aetna, Rowe explicitly sought out informal interactions with employees. These included social visits, ad hoc meetings, impromptu telephone discussions, and e-mail exchanges. He and Williams focused on getting cross-sections of people to reflect on how they were feeling and on identifying their sources of anxiety and concern. Separate nonhierarchical forums among peers and colleagues were also held across the company to discuss Aetna's values—what they were, what they should be, why many of them were no longer being "lived," what needed to happen to resurrect them, and what leadership behaviors would ensure the right employee behaviors.

One early and important networking effort by Rowe was to identify a core group of "key influencers"—potential leaders who could offer invaluable perspectives on the cultural situation, regardless of their level in the hierarchy. Rowe began interacting with a cadre of about 25 influencers and within a few months expanded the group to include close to 100. These discussions not only gave him insights about the staff but created a rapport between him and a respected group that disseminated his message both formally and informally.

5. Measure and Monitor Cultural Evolution

Finally, it's essential to measure and monitor cultural progress at each stage of your effort, just as you would with any other priority business initiative. Rigorous measurement allows executives to identify backsliding, correct course where needed, and demonstrate tangible evidence of improvement—which can help to maintain positive momentum over the long haul.

Executives should pay attention to four areas:

Business performance
Are key performance indicators improving? Are relevant growth targets being reached more frequently? What is happening with less obvious indicators, such as local sales improvements or decreases in customer complaints?

Critical behaviors
Have enough people at multiple levels started to exhibit the few behaviors that matter most? For example, if customer relationships are crucial, do managers update the CRM database on a regular basis?

Milestones
Have specific intervention milestones been reached? For example, has a new policy successfully been implemented? Are people living up to their commitments to key account targets?

Underlying beliefs, feelings, and mindsets
Are key cultural attitudes moving in the right direction, as indicated by the results of employee surveys?

This last area is usually the slowest to show improvement. Most people will shift their thinking only after new behaviors have led to results that matter—and thereby been validated.

When designing cultural metrics, remember that you get what you measure. An overemphasis on quarterly sales results, for example, can trigger inappropriate pressure on valued customer relationships. And if a company, in an effort to become more customer-centric, defines "engage with your client more often" as a critical behavior and measures it in number of calls per week, its staff may make lots of phone calls without increasing business. Similarly, focusing on retention metrics as an indication of overall engagement and job satisfaction may not be as useful—or as important—as what happens to retention of top performers once a cultural initiative gets under way.

Companies should also use their tracking efforts to remind people of their commitment. Some organizations send out a five-or 10-question survey every other week, asking how often particular behaviors have been exhibited. These surveys serve as good a basis for dialogue and act as a simple reinforcement mechanism.

If not approached correctly, measurement efforts can quickly become cumbersome, time-consuming, and expensive. It's better to include a few carefully designed, specific behavioral measurements in existing scorecards and reporting mechanisms, rather than invent extensive new systems and surveys. In some cases, it may also be worth focusing on interactions within key subpopulations—such as midlevel managers or those in business-critical functions—whose own behaviors have a disproportionate impact on the experiences of others or on business success.

Cultural Intervention as the First Resort

All too often, leaders see cultural initiatives as a last resort, except for top-down exhortations to change. By the time they get around to culture, they're convinced that a comprehensive overhaul of the culture is the only way to overcome the company's resistance to major change. Culture thus becomes an excuse and a diversion, rather than an accelerator and an energizer.

But cultural intervention can and should be an early priority—a way to clarify what your company is capable of, even as you refine your strategy. Targeted and integrated cultural interventions, designed around changing a few critical behaviors at a time, can also energize and engage your most talented people and enable them to collaborate more effectively and efficiently.

Coherence among your culture, your strategic intent, and your performance priorities can make your whole organization more attractive to both employees and customers. Because deeply embedded cultures change slowly over time, working with and within the culture you have invariably is the best approach. The overall change effort will be far less jarring for all concerned. Simply put, rather than attacking the heart of your company, you will be making the most of its positive forces as your culture evolves in the right way.

Originally published in July–August 2012. **Reprint** R1207K

How to Build a Culture of Originality

by Adam Grant

IF THERE'S ONE PLACE on earth where originality goes to die, I'd managed to find it. I was charged with unleashing innovation and change in the ultimate bastion of bureaucracy. It was a place where people accepted defaults without question, followed rules without explanation, and clung to traditions and technologies long after they'd become obsolete: the U.S. Navy.

But in a matter of months, the navy was exploding with originality—and not because of anything I'd done. It launched a major innovation task force and helped to form a Department of Defense outpost in Silicon Valley to get up to speed on cutting-edge technology. Surprisingly, these changes didn't come from the top of the navy's command-and-control structure. They were initiated at the bottom, by a group of junior officers in their twenties and thirties.

When I started digging for more details, multiple insiders pointed to a young aviator named Ben Kohlmann. Officers called him a troublemaker, rabble-rouser, disrupter, heretic, and radical. And in direct violation of the military ethos, these were terms of endearment.

Kohlmann lit the match by creating the navy's first rapid-innovation cell—a network of original thinkers who would collaborate to question long-held assumptions and generate new ideas. To start assembling the group, he searched for black sheep: people with a history of nonconformity. One recruit had been fired from a nuclear submarine for disobeying a commander's order.

Another had flat-out refused to go to basic training. Others had yelled at senior flag officers and flouted chains of command by writing public blog posts to express their iconoclastic views. "They were lone wolves," Kohlmann says. "Most of them had a track record of insubordination."

Kohlmann realized, however, that to fuel and sustain innovation throughout the navy, he needed more than a few lone wolves. So while working as an instructor and director of flight operations, he set about building a culture of nonconformity. He talked to senior leaders about expanding his network and got their buy-in. He recruited sailors who had never shown a desire to challenge the status quo and exposed them to new ways of thinking. They visited centers of innovation excellence outside the military, from Google to the Rocky Mountain Institute. They devoured a monthly syllabus of readings on innovation and debated ideas during regular happy hours and robust online discussions. Soon they pioneered the use of 3-D printers on ships and a robotic fish for stealth underwater missions—and other rapid-innovation cells began springing up around the military. "Culture is king," Kohlmann says. "When people discovered their voice, they became unstoppable."

Empowering the rank and file to innovate is where most leaders fall short. Instead, they try to recruit brash entrepreneurial types to bring fresh ideas and energy into their organizations—and then leave it at that. It's a wrongheaded approach, because it assumes that the best innovators are rare creatures with special gifts. Research shows that entrepreneurs who succeed over the long haul are actually more risk-averse than their peers. The hotshots burn bright for a while but tend to fizzle out. So relying on a few exceptional folks who fit a romanticized creative profile is a short-term move that underestimates everyone else. Most people are in fact quite capable of novel thinking and problem solving, if only their organizations would stop pounding them into conformity.

When everyone thinks in similar ways and sticks to dominant norms, businesses are doomed to stagnate. To fight that inertia and drive innovation and change effectively, leaders need sustained original thinking in their organizations. They get it by building a culture

Idea in Brief

What's Possible

We tend to believe that true innovators are a rare breed. But most people are quite capable of original thinking, and leaders can set them up for success by building a culture of nonconformity.

What Gets in the Way

Unfortunately, leaders often fail to do this because they have trouble moving past their flawed assumptions—for instance,

believing that doing fewer things leads to better work, and that strong cultures squash originality.

What to Do

Give employees ways and reasons to generate lots of new ideas (being prolific actually increases quality). Have fellow innovators evaluate the ideas (they do the best job of predicting success). And strike the right balance between cohesion and dissent in your organization (you need both).

of nonconformity, as Kohlmann did in the navy. I've been studying this for the better part of a decade, and it turns out to be less difficult than I expected.

For starters, leaders must give employees opportunities and incentives to generate—and keep generating—new ideas so that people across functions and roles get better at pushing past the obvious. However, it's also critical to have the right people vetting those ideas. That part of the process should be much less democratic and more meritocratic, because some votes are simply more meaningful than others. And finally, to continue generating and selecting smart ideas over time, organizations need to strike a balance between cultural cohesion and creative dissent.

Letting a Thousand Flowers Bloom

People often believe that to do better work, they should do fewer things. Yet the evidence flies in the face of that assumption: Being prolific actually increases originality, because sheer volume improves your chances of finding novel solutions. In recent experiments by Northwestern University psychologists Brian Lucas and Loran Nordgren, the initial ideas people generated were the most conventional. Once they had thought of those, they were free to start dreaming up more-unusual possibilities. Their first 20 ideas were significantly less original than their next 15.

Across fields, volume begets quality. This is true for all kinds of creators and thinkers—from composers and painters to scientists and inventors. Even the most eminent innovators do their most original work when they're also cranking out scores of less brilliant ideas. Consider Thomas Edison. In a five-year period, he came up with the light bulb, the phonograph, and the carbon transmitter used in telephones—while also filing more than 100 patents for inventions that didn't catch the world on fire, including a talking doll that ended up scaring children (and adults).

Of course, in organizations, the challenge lies in knowing when you've drummed up enough possibilities. How many ideas should you generate before deciding which ones to pursue? When I pose this question to executives, most say you're really humming with around 20 ideas. But that answer is off the mark by an order of magnitude. There's evidence that quality often doesn't max out until more than 200 ideas are on the table.

Stanford professor Robert Sutton notes that the Pixar movie *Cars* was chosen from about 500 pitches, and at Skyline, the toy design studio that generates ideas for Fisher-Price and Mattel, employees submitted 4,000 new toy concepts in one year. That set was winnowed down to 230 to be drawn or prototyped, and just 12 were finally developed. The more darts you throw, the better your odds of hitting a bull's-eye.

Though it makes perfect sense, many managers fail to embrace this principle, fearing that time spent conjuring lots of ideas will prevent employees from being focused and efficient. The good news is that there are ways to help employees generate quantity and variety without sacrificing day-to-day productivity or causing burnout.

Think like the enemy

Research suggests that organizations often get stuck in a rut because they're playing defense, trying to stave off the competition. To encourage people to think differently and generate more ideas, put them on offense.

That's what Lisa Bodell of futurethink did when Merck CEO Ken Frazier hired her to help shake up the status quo. Bodell divided Merck's executives into groups and asked them to come up with ways to put the company out of business. Instead of being cautious and sticking close to established competencies, the executives started considering bold new directions in strategy and product development that competitors could conceivably take. Energy in the room soared as they explored the possibilities. The offensive mindset, Carnegie Mellon professor Anita Woolley observes, focuses attention on "pursuing opportunities . . . whereas defenders are more focused on maintaining their market share." That mental shift allowed the Merck executives to imagine competitive threats that didn't yet exist. The result was a fresh set of opportunities for innovation.

Solicit ideas from individuals, not groups

According to decades of research, you get more and better ideas if people are working alone in separate rooms than if they're brainstorming in a group. When people generate ideas together, many of the best ones never get shared. Some members dominate the conversation, others hold back to avoid looking foolish, and the whole group tends to conform to the majority's taste.

Evidence shows that these problems can be managed through "brainwriting." All that's required is asking individuals to think up ideas on their own before the group evaluates them, to get all the possibilities on the table. For instance, at the eyewear retailer Warby Parker, named the world's most innovative company by *Fast Company* in 2015, employees spend a few minutes a week writing down innovation ideas for colleagues to read and comment on. The company also maintains a Google doc where employees can submit requests for new technology to be built, which yields about 400 new ideas in a typical quarter. One major innovation was a revamped retail point of sale, which grew out of an app that allowed customers to bookmark their favorite frames in the store and receive an e-mail about them later.

Since employees often withhold their most unusual suggestions in group settings, another strategy for seeking ideas is to schedule rapid one-on-one idea meetings. When Anita Krohn Traaseth became managing director of Hewlett-Packard Norway, she launched a "speed-date the boss" initiative. She invited every employee to meet with her for five minutes and answer these questions: Who are you and what do you do at HP? Where do you think we should change, and what should we keep focusing on? And what do you want to contribute beyond fulfilling your job responsibilities? She made it clear that she expected people to bring big ideas, and they didn't want to waste their five minutes with a senior leader—it was their chance to show that they could innovate. More than 170 speed dates later, so many good ideas had been generated that other HP leaders implemented the process in Austria and Switzerland.

Bring back the suggestion box

It's a practice that dates back to the early 1700s, when a Japanese shogun put a box at the entrance to his castle. He rewarded good ideas—but punished criticisms with decapitation. Today suggestion boxes are often ridiculed. "I smell a creative idea being formed somewhere in the building," the boss thinks in one *Dilbert* cartoon. "I must find it and crush it." He sets up a suggestion box, and Dilbert is intrigued until a colleague warns him: "It's a trap!!"

But the evidence points to a different conclusion: Suggestion boxes can be quite useful, precisely because they provide a large number of ideas. In one study, psychologist Michael Frese and his colleagues visited a Dutch steel company (now part of Tata Steel) that had been using a suggestion program for 70 years. The company had 11,000 employees and collected between 7,000 and 12,000 suggestions a year. A typical employee would make six or seven suggestions annually and see three or four adopted. One prolific innovator submitted 75 ideas and had 30 adopted. In many companies, those ideas would have been missed altogether. For the Dutch steelmaker, however, the suggestion box regularly led to improvements—saving more than $750,000 in one year alone.

The major benefit of suggestion boxes is that they multiply and diversify the ideas on the horizon, opening up new avenues for innovation. The biggest hurdle is that they create a larger haystack of ideas, making it more difficult to find the needle. You need a system for culling contributions—and rewarding and pursuing the best ones—so that people don't feel their suggestions are falling on deaf ears.

Developing a Nose for Good Ideas

Generating lots of alternatives is important, but so is listening to the right opinions and solutions. How can leaders avoid pursuing bad ideas and rejecting good ones?

Lean on proven evaluators

Although many leaders use a democratic process to select ideas, not every vote is equally valuable. Bowing to the majority's will is not the best policy; a select minority might have a better sense of which ideas have the greatest potential. To figure out whose votes should be amplified, pay attention to employees' track records in evaluation.

At the hedge fund Bridgewater, employees' opinions are weighted by a believability score, which reflects the quality of their past decisions in that domain. In the U.S. intelligence community, analysts demonstrate their credibility by forecasting major political and economic events. In studies by psychologist Philip Tetlock, forecasters are rated on accuracy (did they make the right bets?) and calibration (did they get the probabilities right?). Once the best of these prognosticators are identified, their judgments can be given greater influence than those of their peers.

So, in a company, who's likely to have the strongest track record? Not managers—it's too easy for them to stick to existing prototypes. And not the innovators themselves. Intoxicated by their own "eureka" moments, they tend to be overconfident about their odds of success. They may try to compensate for that by researching

A Syllabus for Innovators

WHEN AVIATOR BEN KOHLMANN set out to build a culture of nonconformity in the U.S. Navy, he found inspiration in many sources. Here's a sampling of the items he recommends to people who want to think more creatively, along with his comments on how they've influenced his own development.

Speeches

"Lead Like the Great Conductors," TED talk by Itay Talgam

Much can be learned from professions we have no understanding of. People are people—and recognizing the commonalities is useful.

"How Great Leaders Inspire Action," TED talk by Simon Sinek

Sinek cracks the code of influence: Deep-seated desire is what inspires followers and builds movements.

Fiction

Ender's Game, by Orson Scott Card

This novel illustrates how tactical and strategic teams can be adaptable—and how genius can emerge at a young age. It's especially apropos reading in the military, where we promote on seniority and not merit.

Dune, by Frank Herbert

A compelling story about insurgency and taking on established powers, Dune explores the ambiguous nature of messianic saviors.

Nonfiction

Being Wrong: Adventures in the Margin of Error, by Kathryn Schulz

We're wrong a lot, and yet we almost never admit it. Schulz helped me critically evaluate my own biases and better understand how people view and portray themselves.

---

customer preferences, but they'll still be susceptible to confirmation bias (looking for information that supports their view and rejecting the rest). Even creative geniuses have trouble predicting with any accuracy when they've come up with a winner.

Research suggests that fellow innovators are the best evaluators of original ideas. They're impartial, because they're not judging their own ideas, and they're more willing than managers to give radical possibilities a chance. For example, Stanford professor Justin Berg found that circus performers who evaluated videos of their peers'

The Hard Thing About Hard Things, by Ben Horowitz

Horowitz doesn't merely talk about how to lead; he's actually lived it. And who doesn't love a guy who starts his chapters with rap lyrics?

The (Mis)behavior of Markets, by Benoit Mandelbrot

Mandelbrot is the father of fractal theory, and his insight into how that plays into the stock market transformed my understanding of luck's role in managerial successes and failures.

Boyd: The Fighter Pilot Who Changed the Art of War, by Robert Coram

When I read this in college, I realized that those who don't toe the party line often have the most impact.

Mindset: The New Psychology of Success, by Carol Dweck

Dweck argues that intelligence is not fixed. My world opened up once I discovered that we can grow into what we want to be.

Letters to a Young Contrarian, by Christopher Hitchens

I'm a person of faith, but I appreciate the way Hitchens incisively questions everything, even faith. I've used his methods many a time to develop contrarian positions and win debates.

TV Shows
Sherlock (BBC series)

Each episode is pure fun—but yields lots of learning at the same time.

---

new acts were about twice as accurate as managers in predicting popularity with audiences.

Make it a contest

Idea competitions can help leaders separate the wheat from the chaff, whether they're sifting through suggestion-box entries or hosting a live innovation event. At Dow Chemical, for example, employees participate in an annual innovation tournament focused on reducing waste and saving energy. The tournament calls for ideas that require an initial investment of no more than $200,000, and those costs must be recoverable within a year. Peers review the submissions, with monetary rewards going to the winners. Innovation researchers Christian Terwiesch and Karl Ulrich report that over more than a decade, the resulting 575 projects have produced an average return of 204% and saved the company $110 million a year.

When an innovation tournament is well designed, you get a large pool of initial ideas, but they're clustered around key themes instead of spanning a range of topics. People spend a lot of time preparing their entries, which can boost quality, but the work happens in a discrete window of time, so the contest is not a recurring distraction.

Thorough evaluation helps to filter out the bad ideas. The feedback process typically involves having a group of subject matter experts and fellow innovators review the submissions, rate their novelty and usefulness, and provide suggestions for improvement.

With the right judges in place, an innovation contest not only leverages the wisdom of the crowd but also makes the crowd wiser. Contributors and evaluators get to learn from other people's successes and failures. Over time, the culture can evolve into one where employees feel confident in their ability to contribute ideas— and develop better taste about what constitutes quality. Because successful innovators earn recognition and rewards, everyone has an incentive to participate.

So start by calling for ideas to solve a problem or seize an opportunity, and then introduce a rigorous process for assessment and feedback. The most promising submissions will make it to the next round, and the eventual winners should get the staff and resources necessary to implement their ideas.

Cultivating Both Cohesion and Dissent

Building a culture of nonconformity begins with learning how to generate and vet ideas, but it doesn't end there. To maintain originality over time, leaders need to keep fighting the pressures against it.

We used to blame conformity on strong cultures, believing they were so cultish and chummy that members couldn't consider diverse views and make wise decisions. But that's not true. Studies of decision making in top management teams show that cohesive groups *aren't* more likely than others to seek consensus, dismiss divergent opinions, and fall victim to groupthink. In fact, members of strong cultures often make better decisions, because they communicate well with one another and are secure enough in their roles to feel comfortable challenging one another.

Here's the evidence on how successful high-tech founders in Silicon Valley built their start-ups: They hired primarily for commitment to the mission, looking for people who would help carry out their vision and live by their values. Founders who looked mainly for technical skill or star potential didn't fare nearly as well. In mature industries, too, research shows that when companies place a strong emphasis on culture, their performance remains more stable.

Yet there's a dark side to strong, cohesive cultures: They can become homogeneous if left unchecked. As leaders continue to attract, select, and retain similar people, they sacrifice diversity in thoughts and values. Employees face intense pressure to fit in or get out. This sameness can be advantageous in predictable environments, but it's a problem in volatile industries and dynamic markets. In those settings, strong cultures can be too insular to respond appropriately to shifting conditions. Leaders have a hard time recognizing the need for change, considering different views, and learning and adapting.

Consider BlackBerry: After disrupting the smartphone market, senior leaders clung to the belief that users were primarily interested in efficient, secure e-mail. They dismissed the iPhone as a music player and a consumer toy, hired like-minded insiders who had engineering backgrounds but lacked marketing expertise, and ultimately failed to create a high-quality web browser and an app-friendly operating system. The result? A major downsizing, a billion-dollar write-off, and a colossal collapse of market share.

So to balance out a strong culture, you also need a steady supply of critical opinions. Even when they're wrong, they're useful—they disrupt knee-jerk consensus, stimulate original thought, and help organizations find novel solutions to problems. In the navy's rapid-innovation cell, the norm is "loyal opposition," says Joshua Marcuse, one of Ben Kohlmann's collaborators in the Pentagon. "Agitating against the status quo is how we contribute to the mission."

In short, make dissent one of your organization's core values. Create an environment where people can openly share critical opinions and are respected for doing so. In the early days of Apple, employees were passionately committed to making the Mac a user-friendly household product. But each year, the Mac team also gave an award to somebody who had challenged Steve Jobs. Every one of those award winners was promoted.

Cohesion and dissent sound contradictory, but a combination of the two is what brings novel ideas to the table—and keeps a strong culture from becoming a cult. Here are some ways to hold these principles in productive tension:

Prioritize organizational values

Give people a framework for choosing between conflicting opinions and allowing the best ideas to win out. When companies fail to prioritize values, performance suffers. My colleague Andrew Carton led a study showing that across hospitals, heart attack readmission rates were lower and returns on assets were higher when leaders articulated a compelling vision—but only if they spelled out no more than four organizational values. The more values they emphasized beyond that, the greater the odds that people interpreted them differently or didn't focus on the same ones.

Values need to be rank-ordered so that when employees face choices between competing courses of action, they know what comes first. At the software company Salesforce.com, trust is explicitly defined as the number one value, above growth and innovation. That communicates a clear message to employees: When working on new software, never compromise data privacy. At the online shoe and clothing retailer Zappos.com, CEO Tony Hsieh prioritizes employee happiness over customer happiness. The airline WestJet identifies safety as its most important value. And at GiveForward, a company that helps people raise money for causes, compassion tops the list. Although media coverage is critical to the company's success, cofounder Ethan Austin notes, "We will not push a story in the media unless we are certain that the customer whose story we are sharing will benefit more than we do."

Once you've prioritized the values, keep scrutinizing them. Encourage new hires to challenge "the company way" when they disagree with it. They're the ones with the freshest perspective; they haven't yet gone native. If they familiarize themselves with the culture before speaking up, they'll have already started marching to the same drummer. At Bridgewater, when new employees are trained, they're asked about the company's principles: Do you disagree?

Solicit problems, not just solutions

When working with executives, organizational psychologist David Hofmann likes to ask them to fill in the blanks in this sentence: "Don't bring me ___; bring me ___." Without fail, they shout out, "Don't bring me *problems*; bring me *solutions!*"

Although leaders love it when employees come up with solutions, there's an unintended consequence: Inquiry gets dampened. If you're always expected to have an answer ready, you'll arrive at meetings with your diagnosis complete, missing out on the chance to learn from a range of perspectives. This may be especially common in the United States: In a recent study comparing American and German decision groups, the Germans made twice as many statements about problems and 30% fewer statements about solutions. "Americans are driven to find solutions quickly," the researchers observe, "often without a complete and thorough analysis of the problem."

When individual members of a group have different information, as is usually the case in organizations, it's smarter to get all the problems out there before pursuing solutions. At the digital music company Spotify, instead of working on projects, people organize around long-term business problems. "If they were easy to solve," chief technology officer Oskar Stål notes, "we would have solved them already. When we create a new team, people typically stay together on a business problem for at least a year. If it becomes successful, the team and mission will exist for a long time." Angie's List cofounder Angie Hicks holds weekly office hours to hear concerns from employees. And when Anita Krohn Traaseth became the CEO of the Norwegian government's innovation efforts, she again used "speed dates" to give employees a voice. To make sure she had full visibility into problems, she asked people to name their three biggest bottlenecks and what they would like to safeguard or change. Only after gathering problems across a tour of 14 offices did she begin implementing solutions.

Don't appoint devil's advocates—go find them

Research by UC Berkeley psychologist Charlan Nemeth shows that assigning someone to play devil's advocate doesn't overcome confirmation bias. Though people may pay lip service to considering the counterargument, they'll stick to their own views in the end.

To make a difference, the devil's advocate has to actually hold a dissenting view, not just voice it for argument's sake, and the group has to believe that the dissent is authentic. Under those circumstances, groups look at more information *against* the majority view than for it, and they're less confident in their original preferences. It's rare that role-played disagreement is forcefully argued or taken seriously; actual disagreement is what stimulates thought.

Groups with authentic dissenters generate more—and better—solutions to problems. Abraham Lincoln famously asked his political rivals to join his cabinet, knowing they would genuinely hold contrarian views. At a recent Berkshire Hathaway annual meeting, Warren Buffett invited a trader who was shorting the stock to share his criticisms. Of course, this strategy works only if the dissenter's input is clearly valued and respected.

Model receptivity to critical feedback

Many managers end up promoting conformity because their egos are fragile. Research reveals that insecurity prevents managers from seeking ideas and leads them to respond defensively to suggestions. Employees quickly pick up on this and withhold ideas to avoid trouble. One way to overcome this barrier is to encourage people to challenge you out in the open.

Years ago at the software company Index Group, CEO Tom Gerrity gathered his full staff of about 100 people and had a consultant give him negative feedback in front of everyone. When employees saw their CEO listen to critical opinions, they were less worried about speaking up. And managers became more receptive to tough comments themselves.

You can also get people to challenge you by broadcasting your weaknesses. "When you're the leader, it is really hard to get good and honest feedback, no matter how many times you ask for it," Facebook COO Sheryl Sandberg says. "One trick I've discovered is that I try to speak really openly about the things I'm bad at, because that gives people permission to agree with me, which is a lot easier than pointing it out in the first place." For example, Sandberg tells her colleagues that she has a habit of talking too much in meetings. "If I never mentioned it, would anyone walk up to me and say, 'Hey, Sheryl, I think you talked too much today'? I doubt it."

––––––––––––––

For a culture of originality to flourish, employees must feel free to contribute their wildest ideas. But they are often afraid to speak up, even if they've never seen anything bad happen to those who do.

To fight that fear in the navy, Ben Kohlmann rejected the military's traditional emphasis on hierarchy. Everyone communicated on a first-name basis, ignoring rank. "If you have an idea, pitch it to the crowd and run with it," he told members of his rapid-innovation cell. And he introduced them to people who had successfully championed creativity and change in the navy, to show them it was possible.

Other ways to nip fear in the bud include applauding employees for speaking up, even when their suggestions don't get adopted, and sharing your own harebrained ideas. Without some degree of tolerance in the organization for bad ideas, conformity will begin to rear its ugly head. Ultimately, listening to a wider range of insights than you normally hear is the key to promoting great original thinking.

If at first you don't succeed, you'll know you're aiming high enough.

Originally published in March 2016. Reprint R1603H

When Culture Doesn't Translate

by Erin Meyer

UNTIL RECENTLY MOST OF US worked in organizations that were largely local. We interacted with colleagues and clients who were with us and culturally like us. Fellow staff members were often in the same building and at the very least were in the same country, which meant that they had similar ways of communicating and making decisions.

But as companies internationalize, their employees become geographically dispersed and lose their shared assumptions and norms. People in different countries react to inputs differently, communicate differently, and make decisions differently. Organically grown corporate cultures that were long taken for granted begin to break down. Miscommunication becomes more frequent, and trust erodes, especially between the head office and the regional units. In their efforts to fix these problems, companies risk compromising attributes that underlie their commercial success.

In the following pages I'll describe the process of cultural disintegration and illustrate how traditional solutions can backfire. I'll conclude with five principles that can help executives prevent disintegration from setting in. Consciously and wisely applying them will lead to a more nuanced understanding of the forces at play, which in itself will increase the chances of success.

Implicit Communication Breaks Down

In companies where everyone is located in the same country, passing messages implicitly is frequently the norm. The closer the space we share and the more similar our cultural backgrounds, the stronger our reliance on unspoken cues. In these settings we communicate in shorthand, often without realizing it—reading our counterparts' tone of voice, picking up on subtext. A manager at Louis Vuitton told me, "At our company, managers didn't finish their sentences. Instead, they would begin to make a point and then say something like 'OK, you get it?' And for us, that said it all."

A lot of work is done in this implicit way without anyone's taking note. If I walk by your office and see you studying October's budget with a worried look, I might send you a comprehensive breakdown of my costs for the month. If I see you shrink in your seat when the boss asks if you can meet a deadline, I know that your "yes" really means "I wish I could," and I might follow you to your office after the meeting to hear the real deal. In such ways we continually adjust to one another's unspoken cues.

But when companies begin to expand internationally, implicit communication stops working. If you don't tell me you need a budget breakdown, I won't send one. If you say yes even though you mean no, I'll think that you agreed. Because we aren't in the same place, we can't read one another's body language—and because we're from different cultures, we probably couldn't read it accurately even if we were within arm's length. The more we work with people from other cultures in far-flung locations, the less we pick up on subtle meaning and the more we fall victim to misunderstanding and inefficiency.

The obvious solution is to put in place multiple processes that encourage employees to recap key messages and map out in words and pictograms who works for whom, with what responsibilities, and who will take which steps and when. For many organizations, that kind of change is largely positive. One banking executive told me, "The more we internationalized, the more we were forced to recap both orally and in writing what was meant and what was understood. And that was good for everybody. We realized that

Idea in Brief

The Problem

Many global corporations suffer from miscommunication and misunderstandings, especially between the head office and regional units. This leads to a breakdown in trust. In trying to prevent those problems, companies often lose a key component of what makes them successful.

The Challenge

How can managers adapt individual employees and the organization as a whole to the realities of working in a global marketplace?

The Approach

Success involves the careful application of five principles:

- Identify the dimensions of difference

- Give everyone a voice

- Protect your most creative units

- Train everyone in key norms

- Be heterogeneous everywhere

---

even among those of us sitting at headquarters, the added repetition meant better understanding and fewer false starts."

One downside, of course, is that companies become more bureaucratic and communication slows down. But that isn't the only cost. At Louis Vuitton, for example, mystery is part of the value proposition and infuses the way people work. Employees are not just comfortable with ambiguity; they embrace it, because they believe it is central to the company's success. One manager told me, "The more we wipe out ambiguity between what was meant and what was heard, the further we wander from that essential mysterious ingredient in our corporate culture that has led to our success."

For companies in beauty, fashion, and other creative industries, the advantages of implicit communication may be particularly strong. But many other types of internationalizing companies have activities that may benefit from letting people leave messages open to interpretation, and they, too, need to think carefully about processes that might erode valuable ambiguity in an effort to improve communication.

Fault Lines Appear

Breakdowns in implicit communication exacerbate the second problem an internationalizing company faces: Employees frequently split into separate camps that have an "us versus them" dynamic.

It's natural to feel trust and empathy for those we see daily and those who think like us. We eat lunch together. We laugh together at the coffee machine. It's hard to feel the same bond with people we don't see regularly, especially when they speak an unfamiliar language and have experienced the world differently. When one New York–based financial institution opened offices in Asia, it struggled to export its highly collaborative culture, in which key decisions involve a great deal of consultation. Despite management's best efforts, the local offices created what one executive described as "overseas cocoons," in which employees shared work and consulted with one another but remained isolated from their colleagues in the United States.

Often headquarters wants to be inclusive but finds that employees' exchanges are hampered by differences in social customs. One Thai manager in the financial firm explained, "In Thai culture, there is a strong emphasis on avoiding mistakes, and we are very group oriented in our decision making. If the Americans want to hear from us on a conference call, they need to send the agenda at least 24 hours in advance so that we can prepare what we'd like to say and get feedback from our peers."

Unfortunately, the Thai manager told me, his U.S. colleagues usually didn't send the agenda until an hour before the call, so his team was unable to prepare. And it struggled to understand what was said during the call, because the U.S. participants spoke too quickly. He also said that the Americans rarely invited comments from the Thais, expecting them to jump into the conversation as they themselves would. But that kind of intervention is not the norm in Thailand, where it is much less common to speak if not invited or questioned. The Thai manager summed up his perspective this way: "They invite us to the meeting, but they don't suggest with their actions that they care what we have to say." The Thai team members ended up just sitting on the phone listening—giving the Americans the impression that they had nothing to contribute or weren't interested in participating.

Corporate Culture Clashes with Local Culture

As companies institute rules about communication and inclusiveness, they often run into a third problem. Consider the Dutch shipping company TNT, which has long put a premium on task-oriented efficiency and egalitarian management. When it moved into China, it found that neither of those values fit with local norms. Its corporate culture gradually became more relationship oriented and more hierarchical, as leaders in Asia adapted their styles to attract local clients and motivate the local workforce.

The problem with that kind of adaptation is that a company's culture is often a key driver of its success. Let's look at L'Oréal. Confrontation and open disagreement are a strong part of its corporate culture. As one manager put it, "At L'Oréal we believe the more we debate openly and the more strongly we disagree in meetings, the closer we get to excellence, the more we generate creativity, and the more we reduce risk."

Yet in many important growth areas for L'Oréal, including Southeast Asia and Latin America, that attitude is in direct opposition to a cultural preference for group harmony. A Mexican employee explained, "In Mexican culture, open disagreement is considered rude, disrespectful, and too aggressive." An Indonesian employee said, "To an Indonesian person, confrontation in a group setting is extremely negative, because it makes the other person lose face. So it's something that we try strongly to avoid in any open manner."

If you believe that your corporate culture is what makes your company great, you might focus on maintaining it in all your offices, even when it conflicts with local practice. This can work for companies with a highly innovative product offering and few or no local competitors. In other words, if your corporate culture has led to extreme innovation and you don't need to understand local consumers, it may be best to ignore local culture in order to preserve the organizational core.

For example, Google believes that its success is largely the result of a strong organizational culture. Part of that culture involves giving employees lots of positive feedback. The company's performance review form begins by instructing managers, "List the things this employee did really well." Only then does it say, "List one thing this person could do to have a bigger impact." When Google moved into France, it learned that in that country, positive words are used sparingly and criticism is provided more strongly. One French manager told me, "The first time I used the Google form to give a performance review, I was confused. Where was the section to talk about problem areas? 'What did this employee do *really* well?' The positive wording sounded over the top." But Google's corporate culture is so strong that it often supersedes local preferences; the French manager added, "After five years at Google France, I can tell you we are now a group of French people who give negative feedback in a very un-French way."

Creating a strong corporate culture that is pretty much the same from Beijing to Brasília makes things easier and more efficient internally. But it carries risks. A company with a strong culture typically hires employees who can fit into that culture and trains them to work and behave in a globally accepted fashion. But if you hire the rare Saudi who will challenge authority figures and encourage him to do so, you may find that his egalitarian directness keeps him from closing deals with local clients and suppliers.

Planning for Your International Culture

As companies internationalize to exploit new opportunities, how can they prevent communication breakdowns, fault lines, and other risks? As with most cultural and organizational dysfunctions, the cures are often less obvious than the symptoms, and the specifics will vary from case to case. Nonetheless, my experience suggests that if companies apply some ground rules carefully, they are more likely to adapt their culture to new countries without losing key strengths.

Identify the dimensions of difference

The first imperative when managing a clash between a corporate culture and a national one is understanding the relevant dimensions along which those cultures vary. Are decisions made by consensus, or does the boss decide? Are timeliness and structure foremost in everyone's mind, or is flexibility at the heart of the company's success? Only after you've figured out where the pressure points are can you make plans for dealing with them.

It's important to perform this analysis along multiple dimensions, because managers tend to boil cultural differences down to one or two features, often causing unexpected problems. (See my May 2014 HBR article, "Navigating the Cultural Minefield.") For instance, French executives expecting straight talk from U.S. colleagues are routinely tripped up by Americans' reluctance to give harsh feedback, while expatriate Americans are often blindsided by their outwardly polite and socially aware French bosses' savage critiques. That said, you can typically reduce the differences you actually have to manage to just three or four dimensions. (For more on how to conduct your analysis, see the "Further Reading" list.)

Give everyone a voice

Although you can vary many rules according to culture and corporate function, the one you absolutely must adopt is ensuring that every cultural group is heard. In practical terms, this involves applying three tenets during meetings and other interactions, especially when people are participating remotely:

- When you invite local offices to phone or video conferences, send the agenda well in advance (not the same day!) and designate a time for those in each location to speak. This allows participants to adequately prepare their comments and double-check them with colleagues.

- Insist that everyone use global English, speaking slowly and clearly, and assign someone to recap the discussion, especially when conversations speed up.

- Check in with international participants every five or 10 minutes and invite them to speak: "Any input from Thailand?" or "Budsaree, did you have any feedback?"

If you follow these basics, you'll go a long way toward preventing people from thinking that their colleagues in other cultures "never speak up because they are hiding information," "have nothing to contribute," or "say they want our input, but act like they don't care what we think."

Protect your most creative units

As your company expands geographically, map out the areas of the organization (usually functional units) that rely heavily on creativity and mutual adjustment to achieve their business objectives. Draw a ring around those areas and let communication within them remain more ambiguous, with flexible job descriptions and meetings that are less predefined.

Elsewhere in the company, where there is no clear benefit to leaving things open to interpretation, go ahead and formalize all systems, processes, and communications. The areas that lend themselves to more-explicit procedures include finance, IT, and production.

You might want to put everything in writing to avoid misperceptions later on. If you don't have an employee handbook, or if your handbook is sometimes vague, you'll need to create a detailed one. But before you start crafting precise job descriptions, make sure you have protected the parts of your company that rely on implicit communication and fluid processes for business success.

Train everyone in key norms

When entering a new market, you'll inevitably have to adapt to some of the local norms. But you should also train local employees to adapt to some of your corporate norms. For example, L'Oréal offers a program called Managing Confrontation, which teaches a methodical approach to expressing disagreement in meetings. Employees around the world hear about the importance of debate for success in the company. A Chinese employee told me, "We don't do this type of debate traditionally in China, but these trainings have taught us a method of expressing diverging opinions which we have all come to practice and appreciate, even in meetings made up of only Chinese."

Exxon Mobil, which prides itself on task-oriented efficiency but has large operations in strongly relationship-oriented societies such as Qatar and Nigeria, reaps tangible benefits from getting employees to adapt to its culture, rather than the other way around. One Qatari employee told me, "The task-oriented mentality gives us a common work platform within the company, so when Texas-based employees are collaborating with Arabs or Brazilians or Nigerians, we all have a similar approach. Cultural differences don't hit us as hard as some companies."

Be heterogeneous everywhere

If 99% of your engineers in Shanghai are Chinese and 99% of your HR experts in London are British, you run a high risk of having fault lines appear. If all the Shanghai employees are in their thirties and all those in London are in their fifties, the rifts may widen. And if almost all the Shanghai employees are men while most of the London employees are women, things may get even worse. Take steps at the start to ensure diversity in each location. Mix the tasks and functions among locations. Instruct staff members to build bridges of cultural understanding.

When BusinessObjects, a company based in France and the United States, expanded into India, cultural differences quickly arose regarding communication up and down the hierarchy. One U.S. manager, Sarah, told me, "I often need information from individuals on Sanjay's staff. I e-mail them asking for input but get no response. The lack of communication is astounding." When I spoke with Sanjay, he said, "Sarah sends e-mails directly to my staff without getting my OK or even copying me. Those e-mails should go to me directly, but she seems to purposefully leave me out of the process. Of course, when my staff receives those e-mails, they are paralyzed."

This relatively minor cultural misunderstanding created tensions aggravated by the fact that all the local employees in Bangalore had spent their entire lives in India; none were in a position to see things from the other perspective. The majority were software engineers in their twenties. And the California office was made up entirely of American midcareer marketing experts, none of whom had ever been to India. A small issue threatened to sink the enterprise.

After holding face-to-face meetings with Sarah's team and Sanjay's, during which the misunderstanding was explained and worked through, BusinessObjects took further steps to get the collaboration back on track. Five engineers from the Indian office were sent to California for six months, and three Americans moved to Bangalore. Some Americans already based in Bangalore were hired for Sanjay's team, and Sarah hired several Indians living in California. Bit by bit the divisiveness decreased and a sense of unity emerged.

Getting culture right should never be an afterthought. Companies that don't plan for how individual employees and the organization as a whole will adapt to the realities of a global marketplace will sooner or later find themselves stumbling because of unnoticed cultural potholes. And by the time they regain their balance, their economic opportunity may have passed.

Further Reading

FOR MORE INSIGHTS on cross-cultural management, see:

- *The Culture Map: Breaking Through the Invisible Boundaries of Global Business*, Erin Meyer, PublicAffairs, 2014

- "Contextual Intelligence," Tarun Khanna, HBR, September 2014

- "Voices from the Front Lines," Luc Minguet, Eduardo Caride, Takeo Yamaguchi, and Shane Tedjarati, HBR, September 2014

- "Navigating the Cultural Minefield," Erin Meyer, HBR, May 2014

- "L'Oréal Masters Multiculturalism," Hae-Jung Hong and Yves Doz, HBR, June 2013

- *Riding the Waves of Culture: Understanding Diversity in Global Business*, Fons Trompenaars and Charles Hampden-Turner, McGraw-Hill, 2012 (3rd edition)

- *Cultures and Organizations: Software of the Mind*, Geert Hofstede, Gert Jan Hofstede, and Michael Minkov, McGraw-Hill, 2010 (3rd edition)

Originally published in October 2015.   Reprint R1510C

Culture Is Not the Culprit

by Jay W. Lorsch and Emily Gandhi

WHEN ORGANIZATIONS get into big trouble, fixing the culture is usually the prescription. That's what most everyone said General Motors needed to do after its recall crisis in 2014—and ever since, CEO Mary Barra has been focusing on creating "the right environment" to promote accountability and head off future disasters. Pundits far and wide called for the same remedy when it came to light that the U.S. Department of Veterans Affairs, deemed a corrosive bureaucracy by federal investigators, kept veterans waiting months for critical health care. Cultural reform has likewise been proposed as the solution to excessive use of force by police departments, unethical behavior in banks, and just about any other major organizational problem you can think of. All eyes are on culture as the cause and the cure.

But the corporate leaders we have interviewed—current and former CEOs who have successfully led major transformations—say that culture isn't something you "fix." Rather, in their experience, cultural change is what you get after you've put new processes or structures in place to tackle tough business challenges like reworking an outdated strategy or business model. The culture evolves as you do that important work.

Though this runs counter to the going wisdom about how to turn things around at GM, the VA, and elsewhere, it makes intuitive sense to look at culture as an outcome—not a cause or a fix. Organizations are complex systems with many ripple effects. Reworking fundamental practices will inevitably lead to some new values and behaviors. Employees may start seeing their contributions to society in a whole new light. This is what happened at Ecolab when CEO Doug Baker pushed decisions down to the front lines to strengthen customer relationships. Or people might become less adversarial toward senior executives—as Northwest employees did after Delta CEO Richard Anderson acquired the airline and got workers on board by meeting their day-to-day needs.

The leaders we spoke with took different approaches for different ends. For example, Alan Mulally worked to break down barriers between units at Ford, whereas Dan Vasella did a fair amount of decentralizing to unleash creative energy at Novartis. But in every case, when the leaders used tools such as decision rights, performance measurement, and reward systems to address their particular business challenges, organizational culture evolved in interesting ways as a result, reinforcing the new direction.

Revisiting their stories provides a richer understanding of corporate transformation and culture's role in it, so we share highlights from our conversations here. Most of these stories involve some aspect of merger integration, one of the most difficult transitions for companies to manage. And they all show, in a range of settings, that culture isn't a final destination. It morphs right along with the company's competitive environment and objectives. It's really more of a temporary landing place—where the organization should be at that moment, if the right management levers have been pulled.

Doug Baker

Doug Baker took over as the CEO of Ecolab, an industrial-cleaning-products company, in 2004. At the time company revenue was $4 billion, and he set out to triple that figure, a highly audacious goal. By 2014 he had completed some 50 acquisitions, most notably buying Nalco, a water treatment company based in Naperville, Illinois. Sales had grown to $14 billion, and the workforce had more than doubled.

Idea in Brief

When organizations get into big trouble, fixing the culture is usually the prescription. That's what most everyone said GM needed to do after its 2014 recall crisis. Cultural reform has likewise been proposed as the solution to the corrosive bureaucracy at the Veterans' Administration, unethical behavior in banks, and the excessive use of force by police. But interviews with successful change makers, conducted by Lorsch and Gandhi, suggest that culture isn't something you "fix." Rather, cultural change is what you get when you put new processes or structures in place to tackle tough business challenges.

Organizations are complex systems with many ripple effects—and reworking fundamental practices will inevitably lead to new values and behaviors. The authors explain how this played out during four major transformations:

- The remake of Ecolab into a diversified corporation three times its original size

- The postbankruptcy merger of Delta and Northwest

- The turnaround of Ford

- Novartis's shift to a diversified healthcare portfolio.

Each firm's CEO took a different approach for a different end. Ecolab's Doug Baker pushed decisions down to the front lines to strengthen customer relationships. Delta's Richard Anderson got airline workers on board by focusing on meeting their needs. Ford's Alan Mulally broke down barriers between units to improve collaboration and efficiency. Novartis's Daniel Vasella decentralized to unleash creative energy. But in every case, when the executives used tools such as decision rights, performance measurement, and reward systems to address their particular business challenges, organizational culture evolved as a result, reinforcing the new direction.

The acquisitions allowed Ecolab to offer a more diverse set of products and services—essentially one-stop shopping—for its customers' cleaning needs. But as it absorbed each new entity, complexity grew. Organizational layers multiplied, and managers became siloed into different offices and units. Key decision makers spent less time interacting with customers and with one another. The expanding bureaucracy was eating into Ecolab's customer-centric culture, and that was hurting the business.

Doug Baker, CEO of Ecolab

Business challenge: Staying connected with customers while tripling in size

Levers pulled: Encouraged more frontline decision making and instituted a more meritocratic reward system

Cultural change: Shift from father-knows-best management to a collaborative and independent workforce

Baker wanted to restore customer focus as a core strength at Ecolab. The company's model was to provide on-site evaluations and training for customers and build them customized portfolios of products and services based on those visits. Many of its clients had worked with the company for years, and it was essential to maintain those strong relationships.

The answer, Baker believed, was to encourage more decision making on the front lines, by carefully training the employees who were closest to customers. The more they learned about all the products and services the company provided, the better equipped they would be to figure out on their own which solutions fit customers' needs.

It may seem risky to push decisions down, but Baker found that the bad calls were caught and fixed faster that way. Eventually, managers began to let go and trust their employees—which was a huge cultural shift. It took time to train employees, and it required constant tweaking and reevaluation as customer preferences and business dynamics changed. But ultimately fostering frontline responsibility allowed Ecolab to stay connected with its customers.

Baker also emphasized the importance of meritocracy in motivating employees to carry out business goals. "People watch who gets promoted," he says. Advancement and other rewards were used to signal the kind of behavior that was valued at the company. Baker found that public acknowledgment mattered even more than financial incentives over time. "What do you call people out for, what do you celebrate, how do people get recognized by their peers? The bonus check is not unimportant, but it is silent and it's not public," he points out. Kudos went to managers who delegated decisions to customer-facing employees and encouraged them to take the lead when they showed initiative.

This was especially critical at the smaller organizations Ecolab acquired. They included a number of private companies that had a "father knows best" style of management: The founders issued the orders, and people followed them. Although that could work in small organizations, it hindered growth and made it difficult to collaborate across divisions at Ecolab.

As frontline employees were rewarded for owning customer relationships and coordinating with one another, a culture of autonomy emerged. (This also freed up senior management time, allowing executives to focus on broader issues.) Once people throughout the ranks felt trusted, they in turn trusted the company more and began to view their work and their mission—to make the world cleaner, safer, and healthier—as real contributions to society. And in their enhanced roles, they could see firsthand how they were making customers' lives better. This shift took time, though, because the process had to happen again and again with each acquisition.

"When we buy businesses, they're not going to love the new company right away," Baker says. "Love takes a while."

Richard Anderson

Soon after he became Delta's CEO, Richard Anderson oversaw the 2008 acquisition of Northwest, which created the world's largest carrier, with approximately 70,000 employees. At the time, both airlines were emerging from bankruptcy protection and entering a major downturn in air travel.

Unlike Baker, who didn't rush postmerger integration, Anderson felt that this acquisition demanded speed and force. He didn't have the time or inclination to do any wooing. "There's no such thing as a merger of equals," he says. "We called all the shots here. It was going to be based in Atlanta; it was going to be called Delta; there was going to be no joint branding. It was pretty dictatorial."

To quickly integrate systems, processes, and people in a hugely complex industry, Anderson had to empower those around him to lead. He

Richard Anderson, CEO of Delta

Business challenge: Quick integration of a giant acquisition during a downturn

Levers pulled: Shared executive power, built more-direct relationships with employees, and focused on accommodating their workplace development and compensation needs

Cultural change: Shift from adversarial management-employee relationship to mutual loyalty and trust

---

firmly believes in having a nonexecutive chairman, who oversees board agendas and processes, and a separate president, who independently manages deals. "The president and I carry the same cachet," Anderson says, "so we can get twice as much done. He can go run the Virgin Atlantic transaction while I'm in China trying to work a deal with our two Chinese partners." Anderson has also delegated a lot of responsibility to his chief operating officer and chief marketing officer.

Because Anderson had previously served as Northwest's CEO for three and a half years, he had an insider's view of the company—and he knew about a major obstacle he would encounter there. Northwest was highly unionized, which in his view set up an adversarial dynamic between employees and management. It also made communication between the two groups difficult. Management relied on unions to learn about employee needs as opposed to interacting with workers directly. With both management and employees going through a third party, it took longer to address issues.

That's why a critical part of this quick integration—once Anderson had clearly laid out that Delta was running the show—was to build strong relationships with employees. So he looked for ways to satisfy them and motivate them to serve the company and its customers. He decided to focus on meeting their needs both on the job and personally. Delta offered employees first-rate training, flexible scheduling, well-maintained airplanes with world-class equipment, and good crew hotels. Those things were relatively inexpensive, especially compared with fuel—and they paid off handsomely in loyalty and trust.

Compensating people well made a difference, too—it motivated them to perform. "You want them to be very productive and work very hard and do everything right," Anderson says, "but in return you want to provide a really good benefit system and a very good pay system." Each year Delta earmarked 10% of its earnings before taxes and management compensation for employee bonuses. One year after the merger, the airline put 15% of the company's equity into a stock-ownership plan for pilots, flight crews, and ground and support staff. The higher compensation demonstrated that management cared about its people, further feeding the culture of trust.

He also recognized that each employee had specific needs. Take the equipment service workers on the second shift. "It's 10 below zero outside in Minneapolis this morning, with a blizzard, and they've got to get their job done," Anderson says. "They've got to get up in the deicing bucket and get that airplane deiced and get off the gate."

The bets that Anderson placed on meeting employee needs seem to have reversed the troubling "us versus management" dynamic. Two years after he took over as CEO, workers voted to get rid of unions (except for pilots, who gain industry influence from being in a union because it puts them on par with their peers at other airlines). Today Delta is the only major airline outside the Middle East that remains largely nonunionized.

The happier workers are, the longer they want to stay. So the company's "lifer" culture has grown even stronger, which Anderson sees as a good thing. "We have a lot of 40- or 45-year employees in this company, and they may be second or third generation," he says. "But we don't have a nepotism rule, because I want generations of the same family working here." His philosophy is that having relatives of employees join Delta tends to increase loyalty all around. Those hires come in with a certain understanding and a positive view of how the company operates.

Alan Mulally

When Alan Mulally took the helm at Ford, in 2006, the company was on the brink of bankruptcy and had lost nearly 25% of its market share since 1990. But, having managed Boeing through a rough downturn, he knew how to make tough calls and act decisively

Alan Mulally, Former CEO of Ford

Business challenge: Bringing a global manufacturer back from the brink of bankruptcy

Levers pulled: Increased transparency among unit heads and streamlined business processes

Cultural change: Shift from defensive and disparate to cooperative and connected business units

---

during a crisis. At his first financial meeting at Ford, he realized that the company was just months away from running out of cash. Mulally reversed the firm's course: By the time he left, in 2014, Ford had been reporting profits for five years, and the stock price had jumped significantly.

The challenge he faced wasn't just financial, though. To set the company straight, he had to get the management team working more collaboratively. It was notorious for being cutthroat and aggressive. Executives from different units hid information from one another instead of sharing it. Mulally says that Ford was like a "bunch of separate companies" when he took over. Each unit made different cars, targeted different markets, and operated independently—all of which reinforced the defensive "turf" mentality and generated enormous waste.

Drawing on his experience at Boeing, Mulally instituted regular meetings where several levels of executives gathered to share updates on their units. They used a color-coded system (green for good, yellow for caution, and red for trouble) to assess Ford's overall performance on a variety of initiatives quickly and holistically.

At the peak of the company's problems, the group met daily. Mulally hoped the meetings would help identify issues before they became intractable and encourage executives to share ideas and support one another. He also wanted to foster personal accountability; managers had to explain the problems they had and the headway they were making.

Mulally also launched "One Ford," a strategy to integrate Ford units around the world so that the company could eliminate waste and streamline processes. He created global heads for manufacturing, marketing, and product development to lead collaboration internationally and simplify operations.

With all executives working openly, as a team, Mulally could more easily identify low-performing brands. He sold off several of Ford's luxury vehicle brands to focus on the production of smaller, energy-efficient vehicles, including the Fiesta and the Focus, which had potential to expand. Ford returned to its original mission of producing quality cars for the masses.

At the beginning, executives were afraid to speak up about problems—they worried that their colleagues would pounce on any sign of vulnerability. In the first several meetings, all the charts were green, but Mulally pushed back: "We lost billions last year, and you're telling me that there is not a problem?" Eventually, a few brave executives started speaking up, and he praised them for their transparency. (One of them was Mark Fields, who would succeed Mulally as CEO.) In time people realized that being honest allowed them to work together and find solutions more quickly, and their charts reflected what was really happening in their units.

Dan Vasella

After Dan Vasella orchestrated the merger between Sandoz and Ciba-Geigy, in 1996, he was named chief executive of the combined company, Novartis. It eventually became the largest producer of pharmaceuticals in the world.

To meet a broader range of customer needs—and better insulate the company—Vasella led the shift from a prescription-drug-based business to a diversified portfolio of health care products. This major transformation required a much more complex organization.

For Vasella, leading change started with a clear sense of purpose at the top. He had a series of early discussions with a small group of senior managers to establish the company's vision and objectives. The chief goal—"to discover, develop, and bring to patients better

Dan Vasella, Former CEO of Novartis

Business challenge: Managing a more diverse portfolio of products and customers

Levers pulled: Articulated a clear vision, goals, and expectations, and decentralized decision making

Cultural change: Shift from narrowly focused and bureaucratic to a customer-centric and performance-minded organization

---

medicines again and again"—spoke directly to the challenge of broadening the company's offerings. To achieve it, Vasella increased spending on research and development during his tenure.

In those meetings, he also clearly spelled out his expectations for employees. They needed to be flexible, for one thing. As a growing company developing new medicines, Novartis would face challenges no one could anticipate, and the team would have to roll with whatever issues came up. And employees had to be accountable and act in the customers' interests.

To that end, Vasella set up clear metrics for gauging performance and ensuring quality across the company's increasingly diverse units and product groups. As Novartis grew, he knew, more people would need to take charge, and a good performance management system would help keep employees focused on the right things. "You also have to make it clear what you won't tolerate," he says. "I will not tolerate bribing. I will not tolerate bad stories internally."

Vasella believed that collaboration and alignment across divisions should not be forced in a growing company, so he decentralized decision making to empower people to do what was best for their own units. He felt that this allowed teams to move faster and to think and act more creatively. "My view was to focus on the outside—on the competition and the customers," he says. "Don't get inhibited or slow down because of concerns about whether you're behaving in a collaborative way with people you don't need to collaborate with for your results."

As the new practices were implemented, Novartis employees became more customer-centric and performance-minded at the same time. "First you have to deliver to your customers what they hope for [better medicines and vaccines]," Vasella says, "and then you can ask for a return for what you deliver." With each organizational change he made, he realized that the company's culture was starting to match the vision he'd outlined in his early meetings with senior executives.

Originally published in April 2016. Reprint R1604H

Conquering a Culture of Indecision

by Ram Charan

DOES THIS SOUND FAMILIAR? You're sitting in the quarterly business review as a colleague plows through a two-inch-thick proposal for a big investment in a new product. When he finishes, the room falls quiet. People look left, right, or down, waiting for someone else to open the discussion. No one wants to comment—at least not until the boss shows which way he's leaning.

Finally, the CEO breaks the loud silence. He asks a few mildly skeptical questions to show he's done his due diligence. But it's clear that he has made up his mind to back the project. Before long, the other meeting attendees are chiming in dutifully, careful to keep their comments positive. Judging from the remarks, it appears that everyone in the room supports the project.

But appearances can be deceiving. The head of a related division worries that the new product will take resources away from his operation. The vice president of manufacturing thinks that the first-year sales forecasts are wildly optimistic and will leave him with a warehouse full of unsold goods. Others in the room are lukewarm because they don't see how they stand to gain from the project. But they keep their reservations to themselves, and the meeting breaks up inconclusively. Over the next few months, the project is slowly strangled to death in a series of strategy, budget, and operational reviews. It's not clear who's responsible for the killing, but it's plain that the true sentiment in the room was the opposite of the apparent consensus.

In my career as an adviser to large organizations and their leaders, I have witnessed many occasions even at the highest levels when silent lies and a lack of closure lead to false decisions. They are "false" because they eventually get undone by unspoken factors and inaction. And after a quarter century of firsthand observations, I have concluded that these instances of indecision share a family resemblance—a misfire in the personal interactions that are supposed to produce results. The people charged with reaching a decision and acting on it fail to connect and engage with one another. Intimidated by the group dynamics of hierarchy and constrained by formality and lack of trust, they speak their lines woodenly and without conviction. Lacking emotional commitment, the people who must carry out the plan don't act decisively.

These faulty interactions rarely occur in isolation. Far more often, they're typical of the way large and small decisions are made—or not made—throughout a company. The inability to take decisive action is rooted in the corporate culture and seems to employees to be impervious to change.

The key word here is "seems," because, in fact, leaders create a culture of indecisiveness, and leaders can break it. The primary instrument at their disposal is the human interactions—the dialogues—through which assumptions are challenged or go unchallenged, information is shared or not shared, disagreements are brought to the surface or papered over. Dialogue is the basic unit of work in an organization. The quality of the dialogue determines how people gather and process information, how they make decisions, and how they feel about one another and about the outcome of these decisions. Dialogue can lead to new ideas and speed as a competitive advantage. It is the single-most important factor underlying the productivity and growth of the knowledge worker. Indeed, the tone and content of dialogue shapes people's behaviors and beliefs—that is, the corporate culture—faster and more permanently than any reward system, structural change, or vision statement I've seen.

Idea in Brief

The single greatest cause of corporate underperformance is the failure to execute. According to author Ram Charan, such failures usually result from misfires in personal interactions. And these faulty interactions rarely occur in isolation, Charan says in this article originally published in 2001. More often than not, they're typical of the way large and small decisions are made (or not made) throughout an organization. The inability to take decisive action is rooted in a company's culture. Leaders create this culture of indecisiveness, Charan says—and they can break it by doing three things: First, they must engender intellectual honesty in the connections between

people. Second, they must see to it that the organization's social operating mechanisms—the meetings, reviews, and other situations through which people in the corporation transact business—have honest dialogue at their cores. And third, leaders must ensure that feedback and follow-through are used to reward high achievers, coach those who are struggling, and discourage those whose behaviors are blocking the organization's progress. By taking these three approaches and using every encounter as an opportunity to model open and honest dialogue, leaders can set the tone for an organization, moving it from paralysis to action.

Breaking a culture of indecision requires a leader who can engender intellectual honesty and trust in the connections between people. By using each encounter with his or her employees as an opportunity to model open, honest, and decisive dialogue, the leader sets the tone for the entire organization.

But setting the tone is only the first step. To transform a culture of indecision, leaders must also see to it that the organization's *social operating mechanisms*—that is, the executive committee meetings, budget and strategy reviews, and other situations through which the people of a corporation do business—have honest dialogue at their center. These mechanisms set the stage. Tightly linked and consistently practiced, they establish clear lines of accountability for reaching decisions and executing them.

Follow-through and feedback are the final steps in creating a decisive culture. Successful leaders use follow-through and honest feedback to reward high achievers, coach those who are struggling, and redirect the behaviors of those blocking the organization's progress.

In sum, leaders can create a culture of decisive behavior through attention to their own dialogue, the careful design of social operating mechanisms, and appropriate follow-through and feedback.

It All Begins with Dialogue

Studies of successful companies often focus on their products, business models, or operational strengths: Microsoft's world-conquering Windows operating system, Dell's mass customization, Wal-Mart's logistical prowess. Yet products and operational strengths aren't what really set the most successful organizations apart—they can all be rented or imitated. What can't be easily duplicated are the decisive dialogues and robust operating mechanisms and their links to feedback and follow-through. These factors constitute an organization's most enduring competitive advantage, and they are heavily dependent on the character of dialogue that a leader exhibits and thereby influences throughout the organization.

Decisive dialogue is easier to recognize than to define. It encourages incisiveness and creativity and brings coherence to seemingly fragmented and unrelated ideas. It allows tensions to surface and then resolves them by fully airing every relevant viewpoint. Because such dialogue is a process of intellectual inquiry rather than of advocacy, a search for truth rather than a contest, people feel emotionally committed to the outcome. The outcome seems "right" because people have helped shape it. They are energized and ready to act.

Not long ago, I observed the power of a leader's dialogue to shape a company's culture. The setting was the headquarters of a major U.S. multinational. The head of one of the company's largest business units was making a strategy presentation to the CEO and a few of his senior lieutenants. Sounding confident, almost cocky, the unit head laid out his strategy for taking his division from number three in Europe to number one. It was an ambitious plan that hinged on making rapid, sizable market-share gains in Germany, where the company's main competitor was locally based and four times his division's size. The CEO commended his unit head for the inspiring and visionary presentation, then initiated a dialogue to test whether the plan was realistic. "Just how are you going to make these gains?" he wondered aloud. "What other alternatives have you considered? What customers do you plan to acquire?" The unit manager hadn't thought that far ahead. "How have you defined the customers' needs in new and unique ways? How many salespeople do you have?" the CEO asked.

"Ten," answered the unit head.

"How many does your main competitor have?"

"Two hundred," came the sheepish reply.

The boss continued to press: "Who runs Germany for us? Wasn't he in another division up until about three months ago?"

Had the exchange stopped there, the CEO would have only humiliated and discouraged this unit head and sent a message to others in attendance that the risks of thinking big were unacceptably high. But the CEO wasn't interested in killing the strategy and demoralizing the business unit team. Coaching through questioning, he wanted to inject some realism into the dialogue. Speaking bluntly, but not angrily or unkindly, he told the unit manager that he would need more than bravado to take on a formidable German competitor on its home turf. Instead of making a frontal assault, the CEO suggested, why not look for the competition's weak spots and win on speed of execution? Where are the gaps in your competitor's product line? Can you innovate something that can fill those gaps? What customers are the most likely buyers of such a product? Why not zero in on them? Instead of aiming for overall market-share gains, try resegmenting the market. Suddenly, what had appeared to be a dead end opened into new insights, and by the end of the meeting, it was decided that the manager would rethink the strategy and return in 90 days with a more realistic alternative. A key player whose strategy proposal had been flatly rejected left the room feeling energized, challenged, and more sharply focused on the task at hand.

Dialogue Killers

IS THE DIALOGUE IN YOUR meetings an energy drain? If it doesn't energize people and focus their work, watch for the following.

Dangling Dialogue

Symptom: Confusion prevails. The meeting ends without a clear next step. People create their own self-serving interpretations of the meeting, and no one can be held accountable later when goals aren't met.
Remedy: Give the meeting closure by ensuring that everyone knows who will do what, by when. Do it in writing if necessary, and be specific.

Information Clogs

Symptom: Failure to get all the relevant information into the open. An important fact or opinion comes to light after a decision has been reached, which reopens the decision. This pattern happens repeatedly.
Remedy: Ensure that the right people are in attendance in the first place. When missing information is discovered, disseminate it immediately. Make the expectation for openness and candor explicit by asking, "What's missing?" Use coaching and sanctions to correct information hoarding.

Piecemeal Perspectives

Symptom: People stick to narrow views and self-interests and fail to acknowledge that others have valid interests.

Think about what happened here. Although it might not have been obvious at first, the CEO was not trying to assert his authority or diminish the executive. He simply wanted to ensure that the competitive realities were not glossed over and to coach those in attendance on both business acumen and organizational capability as well as on the fine art of asking the right questions. He was challenging the proposed strategy not for personal reasons but for business reasons.

The dialogue affected people's attitudes and behavior in subtle and not so subtle ways: They walked away knowing that they should look for opportunities in unconventional ways and be prepared to answer the inevitable tough questions. They also knew that the CEO was on their side. They became more convinced that

Remedy: Draw people out until you're sure all sides of the issue have been represented. Restate the common purpose repeatedly to keep everyone focused on the big picture. Generate alternatives. Use coaching to show people how their work contributes to the overall mission of the enterprise.

Free-for-All

Symptom: By failing to direct the flow of the discussion, the leader allows negative behaviors to flourish. "Extortionists" hold the whole group for ransom until others see it their way; "sidetrackers" go off on tangents, recount history by saying "When I did this ten years ago . . .," or delve into unnecessary detail; "silent liars" do not express their true opinions, or they agree to things they have no intention of doing; and "dividers" create breaches within the group by seeking support for their viewpoint outside the social operating mechanism or have parallel discussions during the meeting.

Remedy: The leader must exercise inner strength by repeatedly signaling which behaviors are acceptable and by sanctioning those who persist in negative behavior. If less severe sanctions fail, the leader must be willing to remove the offending player from the group.

growth was possible and that action was necessary. And something else happened: They began to adopt the CEO's tone in subsequent meetings. When, for example, the head of the German unit met with his senior staff to brief them on the new approach to the German market, the questions he fired at his sales chief and product development head were pointed, precise, and aimed directly at putting the new strategy into action. He had picked up on his boss's style of relating to others as well as his way of eliciting, sifting, and analyzing information. The entire unit grew more determined and energized.

The chief executive didn't leave the matter there, though. He followed up with a one-page, handwritten letter to the unit head stating the essence of the dialogue and the actions to be executed.

And in 90 days, they met again to discuss the revised strategy. (For more on fostering decisive dialogue, see the sidebar "Dialogue Killers.")

How Dialogue Becomes Action

The setting in which dialogue occurs is as important as the dialogue itself. The social operating mechanisms of decisive corporate cultures feature behaviors marked by four characteristics: openness, candor, informality, and closure. Openness means that the outcome is not predetermined. There's an honest search for alternatives and new discoveries. Questions like "What are we missing?" draw people in and signal the leader's willingness to hear all sides. Leaders create an atmosphere of safety that permits spirited discussion, group learning, and trust.

Candor is slightly different. It's a willingness to speak the unspeakable, to expose unfulfilled commitments, to air the conflicts that undermine apparent consensus. Candor means that people express their real opinions, not what they think team players are supposed to say. Candor helps wipe out the silent lies and pocket vetoes that occur when people agree to things they have no intention of acting on. It prevents the kind of unnecessary rework and revisiting of decisions that saps productivity.

Formality suppresses candor; informality encourages it. When presentations and comments are stiff and prepackaged, they signal that the whole meeting has been carefully scripted and orchestrated. Informality has the opposite effect. It reduces defensiveness. People feel more comfortable asking questions and reacting honestly, and the spontaneity is energizing.

If informality loosens the atmosphere, closure imposes discipline. Closure means that at the end of the meeting, people know exactly what they are expected to do. Closure produces decisiveness by assigning accountability and deadlines to people in an open forum. It tests a leader's inner strength and intellectual resources. Lack of closure, coupled with a lack of sanctions, is the primary reason for a culture of indecision.

A robust social operating mechanism consistently includes these four characteristics. Such a mechanism has the right people participating in it, and it occurs with the right frequency.

When Dick Brown arrived at Electronic Data Systems (EDS) in early 1999, he resolved to create a culture that did more than pay lip service to the ideals of collaboration, openness, and decisiveness. He had a big job ahead of him. EDS was known for its bright, aggressive people, but employees had a reputation for competing against one another at least as often as they pulled together. The organization was marked by a culture of lone heroes. Individual operating units had little or no incentive for sharing information or cooperating with one another to win business. There were few sanctions for "lone" behaviors and for failure to meet performance goals. And indecision was rife. As one company veteran puts it, "Meetings, meetings, and more meetings. People couldn't make decisions, wouldn't make decisions. They didn't have to. No accountability." EDS was losing business. Revenue was flat, earnings were on the decline, and the price of the company's stock was down sharply.

A central tenet of Brown's management philosophy is that "leaders get the behavior they tolerate." Shortly after he arrived at EDS, he installed six social operating mechanisms within one year that signaled he would not put up with the old culture of rampant individualism and information hoarding. One mechanism was the "performance call," as it is known around the company. Once a month, the top 100 or so EDS executives worldwide take part in a conference call where the past month's numbers and critical activities are reviewed in detail. Transparency and simultaneous information are the rules; information hoarding is no longer possible. Everyone knows who is on target for the year, who is ahead of projections, and who is behind. Those who are behind must explain the shortfall—and how they plan to get back on track. It's not enough for a manager to say she's assessing, reviewing, or analyzing a problem. Those aren't the words of someone who is acting, Brown says. Those are the words of someone getting ready to act. To use them in front of Brown is to invite two questions in response: When you've finished your analysis, what are you going to do? And how soon are

GE's Secret Weapon

KNOWN FOR ITS STATE-OF-THE-ART management practices, General Electric has forged a system of ten tightly linked social operating mechanisms. Vital to GE's success, these mechanisms set goals and priorities for the whole company as well as for its individual business units and track each unit's progress toward those goals. CEO Jack Welch also uses the system to evaluate senior managers within each unit and reward or sanction them according to their performance.

Three of the most widely imitated of these mechanisms are the Corporate Executive Council (CEC), which meets four times a year; the annual leadership and organizational reviews, known as Session C; and the annual strategy reviews, known as S-1 and S-2. Most large organizations have similar mechanisms. GE's, however, are notable for their intensity and duration; tight links to one another; follow-through; and uninhibited candor, closure, and decisiveness.

At the CEC, the company's senior leaders gather for two-and-a-half days of intensive collaboration and information exchange. As these leaders share best practices, assess the external business environment, and identify the company's most promising opportunities and most pressing problems, Welch has a chance to coach managers and observe their styles of working, thinking, and collaborating. Among the ten initiatives to emerge from these meetings in the past 14 years are GE's Six Sigma quality-improvement drive and its companywide e-commerce effort. These sessions aren't for the fainthearted—at times, the debates can resemble verbal combat. But by the time the CEC breaks up, everyone in attendance knows both what the corporate priorities are and what's expected of him or her.

At Session C meetings, Welch and GE's senior vice president for human resources, Bill Conaty, meet with the head of each business unit as well as his or her top HR executive to discuss leadership and organizational issues. In these intense 12- to 14-hour sessions, the attendees review the unit's prospective talent pool and its organizational priorities. Who needs to be

you going to do it? The only way that Brown's people can answer those questions satisfactorily is to make a decision and execute it.

The performance calls are also a mechanism for airing and resolving the conflicts inevitable in a large organization, particularly when it comes to cross selling in order to accelerate revenue growth. Two units may be pursuing the same customer, for example, or a customer serviced by one unit may be acquired by a customer serviced promoted, rewarded, and developed? How? Who isn't making the grade? Candor is mandatory, and so is execution. The dialogue goes back and forth and links with the strategy of the business unit. Welch follows up each session with a handwritten note reviewing the substance of the dialogue and action items. Through this mechanism, picking and evaluating people has become a core competence at GE. No wonder GE is known as "CEO University."

The unit head's progress in implementing that action plan is among the items on the agenda at the S-1 meeting, held about two months after Session C. Welch, his chief financial officer, and members of the office of the CEO meet individually with each unit head and his or her team to discuss strategy for the next three years. The strategy, which must incorporate the companywide themes and initiatives that emerged from the CEC meetings, is subjected to intensive scrutiny and reality testing by Welch and the senior staff. The dialogue in the sessions is informal, open, decisive, and full of valuable coaching from Welch on both business and human resources issues. As in Session C, the dialogue about strategy links with people and organizational issues. Again, Welch follows up with a handwritten note in which he sets out what he expects of the unit head as a result of the dialogue.

S-2 meetings, normally held in November, follow a similar agenda to the S-1 meeting, except that they are focused on a shorter time horizon, usually 12 to 15 months. Here, operational priorities and resource allocations are linked.

Taken together, the meetings link feedback, decision making, and assessment of the organization's capabilities and key people. The mechanism explicitly ties the goals and performance of each unit to the overall strategy of the corporation and places a premium on the development of the next generation of leaders. The process is unrelenting in its demand for managerial accountability. At the same time, Welch takes the opportunity to engage in followthrough and feedback that is candid, on point, and focused on decisiveness and execution. This operating system may be GE's most enduring competitive advantage.

by another. Which unit should lead the pursuit? Which unit should service the merged entity? It's vitally important to resolve these questions. Letting them fester doesn't just drain emotional energy, it shrinks the organization's capacity to act decisively. Lack of speed becomes a competitive disadvantage.

Brown encourages people to bring these conflicts to the surface, both because he views them as a sign of organizational health and because they provide an opportunity to demonstrate the style of dialogue he advocates. He tries to create a safe environment for disagreement by reminding employees that the conflict isn't personal.

Conflict in any global organization is built in. And, Brown believes, it's essential if everyone is going to think in terms of the entire organization, not just one little corner of it. Instead of seeking the solution favorable to their unit, they'll look for the solution that's best for EDS and its shareholders. It sounds simple, even obvious. But in an organization once characterized by lone heroes and self-interest, highly visible exercises in conflict resolution remind people to align their interests with the company as a whole. It's not enough to state the message once and assume it will sink in. Behavior is changed through repetition. Stressing the message over and over in social operating mechanisms like the monthly performance calls—and rewarding or sanctioning people based on their adherence to it—is one of Brown's most powerful tools for producing the behavioral changes that usher in genuine cultural change.

Of course, no leader can or should attend every meeting, resolve every conflict, or make every decision. But by designing social operating mechanisms that promote free-flowing yet productive dialogue, leaders strongly influence how others perform these tasks. Indeed, it is through these mechanisms that the work of shaping a decisive culture gets done.

Another corporation that employs social operating mechanisms to create a decisive culture is multinational pharmaceutical giant Pharmacia. The company's approach illustrates a point I stress repeatedly to my clients: Structure divides; social operating mechanisms integrate. I hasten to add that structure is essential. If an organization didn't divide tasks, functions, and responsibilities, it would never get anything done. But social operating mechanisms are required to direct the various activities contained within a structure toward an objective. Well-designed mechanisms perform this integrating function. But no matter how well designed, the mechanisms also need decisive dialogue to work properly.

Two years after its 1995 merger with Upjohn, Pharmacia's CEO Fred Hassan set out to create an entirely new culture for the combined entity. The organization he envisioned would be collaborative, customer focused, and speedy. It would meld the disparate talents of a global enterprise to develop market-leading drugs—and do so faster than the competition. The primary mechanism for fostering collaboration: Leaders from several units and functions would engage in frequent, constructive dialogue.

The company's race to develop a new generation of antibiotics to treat drug-resistant infections afforded Pharmacia's management an opportunity to test the success of its culture-building efforts. Dr. Göran Ando, the chief of research and development, and Carrie Cox, the head of global business management, jointly created a social operating mechanism comprising some of the company's leading scientists, clinicians, and marketers. Just getting the three functions together regularly was a bold step. Typically, drug development proceeds by a series of handoffs. One group of scientists does the basic work of drug discovery, then hands off its results to a second group, which steers the drug through a year or more of clinical trials. If and when it receives the Food and Drug Administration's stamp of approval, it's handed off to the marketing people, who devise a marketing plan. Only then is the drug handed off to the sales department, which pitches it to doctors and hospitals. By supplanting this daisy-chain approach with one that made scientists, clinicians, and marketers jointly responsible for the entire flow of development and marketing, the two leaders aimed to develop a drug that better met the needs of patients, had higher revenue potential, and gained speed as a competitive advantage. And they wanted to create a template for future collaborative efforts.

The company's reward system reinforced this collaborative model by explicitly linking compensation to the actions of the group. Every member's compensation would be based on the time to bring the drug to market, the time for the drug to reach peak profitable share, and total sales. The system gave group members a strong incentive to talk openly with one another and to share information freely. But the creative spark was missing. The first few times the drug development group met, it focused almost exclusively on their differences, which were considerable. Without trafficking in clichés, it is safe to say that scientists, clinicians, and marketers tend to have different ways of speaking, thinking, and relating. And each tended to defend what it viewed as its interests rather than the interests of shareholders and customers. It was at this point that Ando and Cox took charge of the dialogue, reminding the group that it was important to play well with others but even more important to produce a drug that met patients' needs and to beat the competition.

Acting together, the two leaders channeled conversation into productive dialogue focused on a common task. They shared what they knew about developing and marketing pharmaceuticals and demonstrated how scientists could learn to think a little like marketers, and marketers a little like scientists. They tackled the emotional challenge of resolving conflicts in the open in order to demonstrate how to disagree, sometimes strongly, without animosity and without losing sight of their common purpose.

Indeed, consider how one dialogue helped the group make a decision that turned a promising drug into a success story. To simplify the research and testing process, the group's scientists had begun to search for an antibiotic that would be effective against a limited number of infections and would be used only as "salvage therapy" in acute cases, when conventional antibiotic therapies had failed. But intensive dialogue with the marketers yielded the information that doctors were receptive to a drug that would work against a wide spectrum of infections. They wanted a drug that could treat acute infections completely by starting treatment earlier in the course of the disease, either in large doses through an intravenous drip or in smaller doses with a pill. The scientists shifted their focus, and the result was Zyvox, one of the major pharmaceutical success stories of recent years. It has become the poster drug in Pharmacia's campaign for a culture characterized by cross-functional collaboration and speedy execution. Through dialogue, the group created a product that neither the scientists, clinicians, nor marketers acting by themselves could have envisioned or executed. And the mechanism that created this open dialogue is now standard practice at Pharmacia.

Follow-Through and Feedback

Follow-through is in the DNA of decisive cultures and takes place either in person, on the telephone, or in the routine conduct of a social operating mechanism. Lack of follow-through destroys the discipline of execution and encourages indecision.

A culture of indecision changes when groups of people are compelled to always be direct. And few mechanisms encourage directness more effectively than performance and compensation reviews, especially if they are explicitly linked to social operating mechanisms. Yet all too often, the performance review process is as ritualized and empty as the business meeting I described at the beginning of this article. Both the employee and his manager want to get the thing over with as quickly as possible. Check the appropriate box, keep up the good work, here's your raise, and let's be sure to do this again next year. Sorry—gotta run. There's no genuine conversation, no feedback, and worst of all, no chance for the employee to learn the sometimes painful truths that will help her grow and develop. Great compensation systems die for lack of candid dialogue and leaders' emotional fortitude.

At EDS, Dick Brown has devised an evaluation and review process that virtually forces managers to engage in candid dialogue with their subordinates. Everyone at the company is ranked in quintiles and rewarded according to how well they perform compared with their peers. It has proved to be one of the most controversial features of Dick Brown's leadership—some employees view it as a Darwinian means of dividing winners from losers and pitting colleagues against one another.

That isn't the objective of the ranking system, Brown insists. He views the ranking process as the most effective way to reward the company's best performers and show laggards where they need to improve. But the system needs the right sort of dialogue to make it work as intended and serve its purpose of growing the talent pool. Leaders must give honest feedback to their direct reports, especially to those who find themselves at the bottom of the rankings.

Brown recalls one encounter he had shortly after the first set of rankings was issued. An employee who had considered himself one of EDS's best performers was shocked to find himself closer to the bottom of the roster than the top. "How could this be?" the employee asked. "I performed as well this year as I did last year, and last year my boss gave me a stellar review." Brown replied that he could think of two possible explanations. The first was that the employee wasn't as good at his job as he thought he was. The second possibility was that even if the employee was doing as good a job as he did the previous year, his peers were doing better. "If you're staying the same," Brown concluded, "you're falling behind."

That exchange revealed the possibility—the likelihood, even— that the employee's immediate superior had given him a less-than-honest review the year before rather than tackle the unpleasant task of telling him where he was coming up short. Brown understands why a manager might be tempted to duck such a painful conversation. Delivering negative feedback tests the strength of a leader. But critical feedback is part of what Brown calls "the heavy lifting of leadership." Avoiding it, he says, "sentences the organization to mediocrity." What's more, by failing to provide honest feedback, leaders cheat their people by depriving them of the information they need to improve.

Feedback should be many things—candid; constructive; relentlessly focused on behavioral performance, accountability, and execution. One thing it shouldn't be is surprising. "A leader should be constructing his appraisal all year long," Brown says, "and giving his appraisal all year long. You have 20, 30, 60 opportunities a year to share your observations. Don't let those opportunities pass. If, at the end of the year, someone is truly surprised by what you have to say, that's a failure of leadership."

———

Ultimately, changing a culture of indecision is a matter of leadership. It's a matter of asking hard questions: How robust and effective are our social operating mechanisms? How well are they linked? Do they have the right people and the right frequency? Do they have a rhythm and operate consistently? Is follow-through built in? Are rewards and sanctions linked to the outcomes of the decisive dialogue? Most important, how productive is the dialogue within these mechanisms? Is our dialogue marked by openness, candor, informality, and closure?

Transforming a culture of indecision is an enormous and demanding task. It takes all the listening skills, business acumen, and operational experience that a corporate leader can summon. But just as important, the job demands emotional fortitude, follow-through, and inner strength. Asking the right questions; identifying and resolving conflicts; providing candid, constructive feedback; and differentiating people with sanctions and rewards is never easy. Frequently, it's downright unpleasant. No wonder many senior executives avoid the task. In the short term, they spare themselves considerable emotional wear and tear. But their evasion sets the tone for an organization that can't share intelligence, make decisions, or face conflicts, much less resolve them. Those who evade miss the very point of effective leadership. Leaders with the strength to insist on honest dialogue and follow-through will be rewarded not only with a decisive organization but also with a workforce that is energized, empowered, and engaged.

Originally published in April 2001. Reprint R0601J

Radical Change, the Quiet Way

by Debra E. Meyerson

AT ONE POINT OR ANOTHER, many managers experience a pang of conscience—a yearning to confront the basic or hidden assumptions, interests, practices, or values within an organization that they feel are stodgy, unfair, even downright wrong. A vice president wishes that more people of color would be promoted. A partner at a consulting firm thinks new MBAs are being so overworked that their families are hurting. A senior manager suspects his company, with some extra cost, could be kinder to the environment. Yet many people who want to drive changes like these face an uncomfortable dilemma. If they speak out too loudly, resentment builds toward them; if they play by the rules and remain silent, resentment builds inside them. Is there any way, then, to rock the boat without falling out of it?

Over the past 15 years, I have studied hundreds of professionals who spend the better part of their work lives trying to answer this question. Each one of the people I've studied differs from the organizational status quo in some way—in values, race, gender, or sexual preference, perhaps (see the sidebar "How the Research Was Done"). They all see things a bit differently from the "norm." But despite feeling at odds with aspects of the prevailing culture, they genuinely like their jobs and want to continue to succeed in them, to effectively use their differences as the impetus for constructive change. They believe that direct, angry confrontation will get them

How the Research Was Done

THIS ARTICLE IS BASED ON a multipart research effort that I began in 1986 with Maureen Scully, a professor of management at the Center for Gender in Organizations at Simmons Graduate School of Management in Boston. We had observed a number of people in our own occupation—academia—who, for various reasons, felt at odds with the prevailing culture of their institutions. Initially, we set out to understand how these individuals sustained their sense of self amid pressure to conform and how they managed to uphold their values without jeopardizing their careers. Eventually, this research broadened to include interviews with individuals in a variety of organizations and occupations: business people, doctors, nurses, lawyers, architects, administrators, and engineers at various levels of seniority in their organizations.

Since 1986, I have observed and interviewed dozens of tempered radicals in many occupations and conducted focused research with 236 men and women, ranging from midlevel professionals to CEOs. The sample was diverse, including people of different races, nationalities, ages, religions, and sexual orientations, and people who hold a wide range of values and change agendas. Most of these people worked in one of three publicly traded corporations—a financial services organization, a high-growth computer components corporation, and a company that makes and sells consumer products. In this portion of the research, I set out to learn more about the challenges tempered radicals face and discover their strategies for surviving, thriving, and fomenting change. The sum of this research resulted in the spectrum of strategies described in this article.

---

nowhere, but they don't sit by and allow frustration to fester. Rather, they work quietly to challenge prevailing wisdom and gently provoke their organizational cultures to adapt. I call such change agents *tempered radicals* because they work to effect significant changes in moderate ways.

In so doing, they exercise a form of leadership within organizations that is more localized, more diffuse, more modest, and less visible than traditional forms—yet no less significant. In fact, top executives seeking to institute cultural or organizational change—who are, perhaps, moving tradition-bound organizations down new roads or who are concerned about reaping the full potential of marginalized employees—might do well to seek out these tempered radicals, who may be hidden deep within their own organizations.

Idea in Brief

How do you rock your corporate boat—without falling out? You know your firm needs constructive change, but here's your dilemma: If you push your agenda too hard, resentment builds against you. If you remain silent, resentment builds inside you.

What's a manager to do? Become a **tempered radical**—an informal leader who quietly challenges prevailing wisdom and provokes cultural transformation. These radicals bear no banners and sound no trumpets. Their seemingly innocuous changes barely inspire notice. But like steady drops of water, they gradually erode granite.

Tempered radicals embody contrasts. Their commitments are firm, but their means flexible. They yearn for rapid change, but trust in patience. They often work alone, yet unite others. Rather than pressing their agendas, they start conversations. And instead of battling powerful foes, they seek powerful friends. The overall effect? Evolutionary—but relentless—change.

Because such individuals are both dedicated to their companies and masters at changing organizations at the grassroots level, they can prove extremely valuable in helping top managers to identify fundamental causes of discord, recognize alternative perspectives, and adapt to changing needs and circumstances. In addition, tempered radicals, given support from above and a modicum of room to experiment, can prove to be excellent leaders. (For more on management's role in fostering tempered radicals, see the sidebar "Tempered Radicals as Everyday Leaders.")

Since the actions of tempered radicals are not, by design, dramatic, their leadership may be difficult to recognize. How, then, do people who run organizations, who want to nurture this diffuse source of cultural adaptation, find and develop these latent leaders? One way is to appreciate the variety of modes in which tempered radicals operate, learn from them, and support their efforts.

To navigate between their personal beliefs and the surrounding cultures, tempered radicals draw principally on a spectrum of incremental approaches, including four I describe here. I call these *disruptive self-expression, verbal jujitsu, variable-term opportunism,* and *strategic alliance building.* Disruptive self-expression, in which an individual

Idea in Practice

Tempered radicals use these tactics:

Disruptive Self-Expression

Demonstrate your values through your language, dress, office decor, or behavior. People notice and talk—often becoming brave enough to try the change themselves. The more people talk, the greater the impact.

Example: Stressed-out manager John Ziwak began arriving at work earlier so he could leave by 6:00 p.m. to be with family. He also refused evening business calls. As his stress eased, his performance improved. Initially skeptical, colleagues soon accommodated, finding more efficient ways of working and achieving balance in their own lives.

Verbal Jujitsu

Redirect negative statements or actions into positive change.

Example: Sales manager Brad Williams noticed that the new marketing director's peers ignored her during meetings. When one of them co-opted a thought she had already expressed, Williams said: "I'm glad George picked up on Sue's concerns. Sue, did George correctly capture what you were thinking?" No one ignored Sue again.

Variable-Term Opportunism

Be ready to capitalize on unexpected opportunities for short-term change, as well as orchestrate deliberate, longer-term change.

simply acts in a way that feels personally right but that others notice, is the most inconspicuous way to initiate change. Verbal jujitsu turns an insensitive statement, action, or behavior back on itself. Variable-term opportunists spot, create, and capitalize on short- and long-term opportunities for change. And with the help of strategic alliances, an individual can push through change with more force.

Each of these approaches can be used in many ways, with plenty of room for creativity and wit. Self-expression can be done with a whisper; an employee who seeks more racial diversity in the ranks might wear her dashiki to company parties. Or it can be done with a roar; that same employee might wear her dashiki to the office every day. Similarly, a person seeking stricter environmental policies might build an alliance by enlisting the help of one person, the more

Example: Senior executive Jane Adams joined a company with a dog-eat-dog culture. To insinuate her collaborative style, she shared power with direct reports, encouraged them to also delegate, praised them publicly, and invited them to give high-visibility presentations. Her division gained repute as an exceptional training ground for building experience, responsibility, and confidence.

Strategic Alliance Building

Gain clout by working with allies. Enhance your legitimacy and implement change more quickly and directly than you could alone. Don't make "opponents" enemies—they're often your best source of support and resources.

Example: Paul Wielgus started a revolution in his bureaucratic global spirits company—by persuading the opposition to join him. Others derided the training department Wielgus formed to boost employee creativity, and an auditor scrutinized the department for unnecessary expense. Rather than getting defensive, Paul treated the auditor as an equal and sold him on the program's value. The training spread, inspiring employees and enhancing productivity throughout the company.

powerful the better. Or he might post his stance on the company intranet and actively seek a host of supporters. Taken together, the approaches form a continuum of choices from which tempered radicals draw at different times and in various circumstances.

But before looking at the approaches in detail, it's worth reconsidering, for a moment, the ways in which cultural change happens in the workplace.

How Organizations Change

Research has shown that organizations change primarily in two ways: through drastic action and through evolutionary adaptation. In the former case, change is discontinuous and often forced on the

Tempered Radicals as Everyday Leaders

IN THE COURSE OF THEIR DAILY actions and interactions, tempered radicals teach important lessons and inspire change. In so doing, they exercise a form of leadership within organizations that is less visible than traditional forms—but just as important.

The trick for organizations is to locate and nurture this subtle form of leadership. Consider how Barry Coswell, a conservative, yet open-minded lawyer who headed up the securities division of a large, distinguished financial services firm, identified, protected, and promoted a tempered radical within his organization. Dana, a left-of-center, first-year attorney, came to his office on her first day of work after having been fingerprinted—a standard practice in the securities industry. The procedure had made Dana nervous: What would happen when her new employer discovered that she had done jail time for participating in a 1960s-era civil rights protest? Dana quickly understood that her only hope of survival was to be honest about her background and principles. Despite the difference in their political proclivities, she decided to give Barry the benefit of the doubt. She marched into his office and confessed to having gone to jail for sitting in front of a bus.

"I appreciate your honesty," Barry laughed, "but unless you've broken a securities law, you're probably okay." In return for her small confidence, Barry shared stories of his own about growing up in a poor county and about his life in the military. The story swapping allowed them to put aside ideological disagreements and to develop a deep respect for each other. Barry sensed a

organization or mandated by top management in the wake of major technological innovations, by a scarcity or abundance of critical resources, or by sudden changes in the regulatory, legal, competitive, or political landscape. Under such circumstances, change may happen quickly and often involves significant pain. Evolutionary change, by contrast, is gentle, incremental, decentralized, and over time produces a broad and lasting shift with less upheaval.

The power of evolutionary approaches to promote cultural change is the subject of frequent discussion. For instance, in "We Don't Need Another Hero" (HBR, September 2001), Joseph L. Badaracco, Jr., asserts that the most effective moral leaders often operate beneath the radar, achieving their reforms without widespread notice. Likewise, tempered radicals gently and continually push against prevailing norms, making a difference in small but steady ways and budding organizational leader in Dana. Here was a woman who operated on the strength of her convictions and was honest about it but was capable of discussing her beliefs without self-righteousness. She didn't pound tables. She was a good conversationalist. She listened attentively. And she was able to elicit surprising confessions from him.

Barry began to accord Dana a level of protection, and he encouraged her to speak her mind, take risks, and most important, challenge his assumptions. In one instance, Dana spoke up to defend a female junior lawyer who was being evaluated harshly and, Dana believed, inequitably. Dana observed that different standards were being applied to male and female lawyers, but her colleagues dismissed her "liberal" concerns. Barry cast a glance at Dana, then said to the staff, "Let's look at this and see if we are being too quick to judge." After the meeting, Barry and Dana held a conversation about double standards and the pervasiveness of bias. In time, Barry initiated a policy to seek out minority legal counsel, both in-house and at outside legal firms. And Dana became a senior vice president.

In Barry's ability to recognize, mentor, and promote Dana there is a key lesson for executives who are anxious to foster leadership in their organizations. It suggests that leadership development may not rest with expensive external programs or even with the best intentions of the human resources department. Rather it may rest with the open-minded recognition that those who appear to rock the boat may turn out to be the most effective captains.

setting examples from which others can learn. The changes they inspire are so incremental that they barely merit notice—which is exactly why they work so well. Like drops of water, these approaches are innocuous enough in themselves. But over time and in accumulation, they can erode granite.

Consider, for example, how a single individual slowly—but radically—altered the face of his organization. Peter Grant[1] was a black senior executive who held some 18 positions as he moved up the ladder at a large West Coast bank. When he first joined the company as a manager, he was one of only a handful of people of color on the professional staff. Peter had a private, long-term goal: to bring more women and racial minorities into the fold and help them succeed. Throughout his 30-year career running the company's local banks, regional offices, and corporate operations, one of his chief responsibilities was to hire new talent. Each time he had the opportunity, Peter attempted to hire a highly qualified member of a minority. But he did more than that—every time he hired someone, he asked that person to do the same. He explained to the new recruits the importance of hiring women and people of color and why it was their obligation to do likewise.

Whenever minority employees felt frustrated by bias, Peter would act as a supportive mentor. If they threatened to quit, he would talk them out of it. "I know how you feel, but think about the bigger picture here," he'd say. "If you leave, nothing here will change." His example inspired viral behavior in others. Many stayed and hired other minorities; those who didn't carried a commitment to hire minorities into their new companies. By the time Peter retired, more than 3,500 talented minority and female employees had joined the bank.

Peter was the most tempered, yet the most effective, of radicals. For many years, he endured racial slurs and demeaning remarks from colleagues. He waited longer than his peers for promotions; each time he did move up he was told the job was too big for him and he was lucky to have gotten it. "I worked my rear end off to make them comfortable with me," he said, late in his career. "It wasn't *luck*." He was often angry, but lashing out would have been the path of least emotional resistance. So without attacking the system, advancing a bold vision, or wielding great power, Peter chipped away at the organization's demographic base using the full menu of change strategies described below.

Disruptive Self-Expression

At the most tempered end of the change continuum is the kind of self-expression that quietly disrupts others' expectations. Whether waged as a deliberate act of protest or merely as a personal demonstration of one's values, disruptive self-expression in language, dress, office decor, or behavior can slowly change the atmosphere at work. Once people take notice of the expression, they begin to talk about it. Eventually, they may feel brave enough to try the same thing themselves. The more people who talk about the transgressive act or repeat it, the greater the cultural impact.

Consider the case of John Ziwak, a manager in the business development group of a high-growth computer components company. As a hardworking business school graduate who'd landed a plum job, John had every intention of working 80-hour weeks on the fast track to the top. Within a few years, he married a woman who also held a demanding job; soon, he became the father of two. John found his life torn between the competing responsibilities of home and work. To balance the two, John shifted his work hours—coming into the office earlier in the morning so that he could leave by 6 p.m. He rarely scheduled late-afternoon meetings and generally refused to take calls at home in the evening between 6:30 and 9. As a result, his family life improved, and he felt much less stress, which in turn improved his performance at work.

At first, John's schedule raised eyebrows; availability was, after all, an unspoken key indicator of commitment to the company. "If John is unwilling to stay past 6," his boss wondered, "is he really committed to his job? Why should I promote him when others are willing and able to work all the time?" But John always met his performance expectations, and his boss didn't want to lose him. Over time, John's colleagues adjusted to his schedule. No one set up conference calls or meetings involving him after 5. One by one, other employees began adopting John's "6 o'clock rule"; calls at home, particularly during dinner hour, took place only when absolutely necessary. Although the 6 o'clock rule was never formalized, it nonetheless became par for the course in John's department. Some of John's colleagues continued to work late, but they all appreciated these changes in work practice and easily accommodated them. Most people in the department felt more, not less, productive during the day as they adapted their work habits to get things done more efficiently—for example, running meetings on schedule and monitoring interruptions in their day. According to John's boss, the employees appreciated the newfound balance in their lives, and productivity in the department did not suffer in the least.

Tempered radicals know that even the smallest forms of disruptive self-expression can be exquisitely powerful. The story of Dr. Frances Conley offers a case in point. By 1987, Dr. Conley had already established herself as a leading researcher and neurosurgeon at Stanford Medical School and the Palo Alto Veteran's Administration hospital. But as one of very few women in the profession, she struggled daily to maintain her feminine identity in a macho profession and her integrity amid gender discrimination. She had to keep her cool when, for example, in the middle of directing a team of residents through complicated brain surgery, a male colleague would stride into the operating room to say, "Move over, honey." "Not only did that undermine my authority and expertise with the team," Dr. Conley recalled later, "but it was unwarranted—and even dangerous. That kind of thing would happen all the time."

Despite the frustration and anger she felt, Dr. Conley at that time had no intention of making a huge issue of her gender. She didn't want the fact that she was a woman to compromise her position, or vice versa. So she expressed herself in all sorts of subtle ways, including in what she wore. Along with her green surgical scrubs, she donned white lace ankle socks—an unequivocal expression of her femininity. In itself, wearing lace ankle socks could hardly be considered a Gandhian act of civil disobedience. The socks merely said, "I can be a neurosurgeon and be feminine." But they spoke loudly enough in the stolid masculinity of the surgical environment, and, along with other small actions on her part, they sparked conversation in the hospital. Nurses and female residents frequently commented on Dr. Conley's style. "She is as demanding as any man and is not afraid to take them on," they would say, in admiration. "But she is also a woman and not ashamed of it."

Ellen Thomas made a comparable statement with her hair. As a young African-American consultant in a technical services business, she navigated constantly between organizational pressures to fit in and her personal desire to challenge norms that made it difficult for her to be herself. So from the beginning of her employment, Ellen expressed herself by wearing her hair in neat cornrow braids. For

Ellen, the way she wore her hair was not just about style; it was a symbol of her racial identity.

Once, before making an important client presentation, a senior colleague advised Ellen to unbraid her hair "to appear more professional." Ellen was miffed, but she didn't respond. Instead, she simply did not comply. Once the presentation was over and the client had been signed, she pulled her colleague aside. "I want you to know why I wear my hair this way," she said calmly. "I'm a black woman, and I happen to like the style. And as you just saw," she smiled, "my hairstyle has nothing to do with my ability to do my job."

Does leaving work at 6 p.m. or wearing lacy socks or cornrows force immediate change in the culture? Of course not; such acts are too modest. But disruptive self-expression does do two important things. First, it reinforces the tempered radical's sense of the importance of his or her convictions. These acts are self-affirming. Second, it pushes the status quo door slightly ajar by introducing an alternative modus operandi. Whether they are subtle, unspoken, and recognizable by only a few or vocal, visible, and noteworthy to many, such acts, in aggregation, can provoke real reform.

Verbal Jujitsu

Like most martial arts, jujitsu involves taking a force coming at you and redirecting it to change the situation. Employees who practice verbal jujitsu react to undesirable, demeaning statements or actions by turning them into opportunities for change that others will notice.

One form of verbal jujitsu involves calling attention to the opposition's own rhetoric. I recall a story told by a man named Tom Novak, an openly gay executive who worked in the San Francisco offices of a large financial services institution. As Tom and his colleagues began seating themselves around a table for a meeting in a senior executive's large office, the conversation briefly turned to the topic of the upcoming Gay Freedom Day parade and to so-called gay lifestyles in general. Joe, a colleague, said loudly, "I can appreciate that some

A Spectrum of Tempered Change Strategies

THE TEMPERED RADICAL'S SPECTRUM of strategies is anchored on the left by *disruptive self-expression:* subtle acts of private, individual style. A slightly more public form of expression, *verbal jujitsu,* turns the opposition's negative expression or behavior into opportunities for change. Further along the spectrum, the tempered radical uses *variable-term opportunism* to recognize and act on short- and long-term chances to motivate others. And through *strategic alliance building,* the individual works directly with others to bring about more extensive change. The more conversations an individual's action inspires and the more people it engages, the stronger the impetus toward change becomes.

In reality, people don't apply the strategies in the spectrum sequentially or even necessarily separately. Rather, these tools blur and overlap. Tempered radicals remain flexible in their approach, "heating up" or "cooling off" each as conditions warrant.

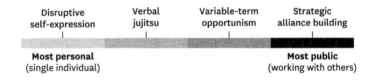

people choose a gay lifestyle. I just don't understand why they have to flaunt it in people's faces."

Stung, Tom was tempted to keep his mouth shut and absorb the injury, but that would have left him resentful and angry. He could have openly condemned Joe's bias, but that would have made him look defensive and self-righteous. Instead, he countered Joe with an altered version of Joe's own argument, saying calmly, "I know what you mean, Joe. I'm just wondering about that big picture of your wife on your desk. There's nothing wrong with being straight, but it seems that you are the one announcing your sexuality." Suddenly embarrassed, Joe responded with a simple, "Touché."

Managers can use verbal jujitsu to prevent talented employees, and their valuable contributions, from becoming inadvertently marginalized. That's what happened in the following story. Brad

Williams was a sales manager at a high-technology company. During a meeting one day, Brad noticed that Sue, the new marketing director, had tried to interject a few comments, but everything she said was routinely ignored. Brad waited for the right moment to correct the situation. Later on in the meeting, Sue's colleague George raised similar concerns about distributing the new business's products outside the country. The intelligent remark stopped all conversation. During the pause, Brad jumped in: "That's an important idea," he said. "I'm glad George picked up on Sue's concerns. Sue, did George correctly capture what you were thinking?"

With this simple move, Brad accomplished a number of things. First, by indirectly showing how Sue had been silenced and her idea co-opted, he voiced an unspoken fact. Second, by raising Sue's visibility, he changed the power dynamic in the room. Third, his action taught his colleagues a lesson about the way they listened—and didn't. Sue said that after that incident she was no longer passed over in staff meetings.

In practicing verbal jujitsu, both Tom and Brad displayed considerable self-control and emotional intelligence. They listened to and studied the situation at hand, carefully calibrating their responses to disarm without harming. In addition, they identified the underlying issues (sexual bias, the silencing of newcomers) without sounding accusatory and relieved unconscious tensions by voicing them. In so doing, they initiated small but meaningful changes in their colleagues' assumptions and behavior.

Variable-Term Opportunism

Like jazz musicians, who build completely new musical experiences from old standards as they go along, tempered radicals must be creatively open to opportunity. In the short term, that means being prepared to capitalize on serendipitous circumstances; in the long term, it often means something more proactive. The first story that follows illustrates the former case; the second is an example of the latter.

Tempered radicals like Chris Morgan know that rich opportunities for reform can often appear suddenly, like a $20 bill found on a sidewalk. An investment manager in the audit department of a New York conglomerate, Chris made a habit of doing whatever he could to reduce waste. To save paper, for example, he would single-space his documents and put them in a smaller font before pressing the "Print" button, and he would use both sides of the paper. One day, Chris noticed that the company cafeteria packaged its sandwiches in Styrofoam boxes that people opened and immediately tossed. He pulled the cafeteria manager aside. "Mary," he said with a big smile, "those turkey-on-focaccia sandwiches look delicious today! I was wondering, though . . . would it be possible to wrap sandwiches only when people asked you to?" By making this very small change, Chris pointed out, the cafeteria would save substantially on packaging costs.

Chris gently rocked the boat by taking the following steps. First, he picked low-hanging fruit, focusing on something that could be done easily and without causing a lot of stir. Next, he attacked the problem not by criticizing Mary's judgment but by enrolling her in his agenda (praising her tempting sandwiches, then making a gentle suggestion). Third, he illuminated the advantages of the proposed change by pointing out the benefits to the cafeteria. And he started a conversation that, through Mary, spread to the rest of the cafeteria staff. Finally, he inspired others to action: Eventually, the cafeteria staff identified and eliminated 12 other wasteful practices.

Add up enough conversations and inspire enough people and, sooner or later, you get real change. A senior executive named Jane Adams offers a case in point. Jane was hired in 1995 to run a 100-person, mostly male software-development division in an extremely fast-growing, pre-IPO technology company. The CEO of the company was an autocrat who expected his employees to emulate his dog-eat-dog management style. Although Jane was new to the job and wanted very much to fit in and succeed, turf wars and command-and-control tactics were anathema to her. Her style was more collaborative; she believed in sharing power. Jane knew that she could not attack the company's culture by arguing with the CEO;

rather, she took charge of her own division and ran it her own way. To that end, she took every opportunity to share power with subordinates. She instructed each of her direct reports to delegate responsibility as much as possible. Each time she heard about someone taking initiative in making a decision, she would praise that person openly before his or her manager. She encouraged people to take calculated risks and to challenge her.

When asked to give high-visibility presentations to the company's executive staff, she passed the opportunities to those who had worked directly on the project. At first, senior executives raised their eyebrows, but Jane assured them that the presenter would deliver. Thus, her subordinates gained experience and won credit that, had they worked for someone else, they would likely never have received.

Occasionally, people would tell Jane that they noticed a refreshing contrast between her approach and the company's prevailing one. "Thanks, I'm glad you noticed," she would say with a quiet smile. Within a year, she saw that several of her own direct reports began themselves to lead in a more collaborative manner. Soon, employees from other divisions, hearing that Jane's was one of the best to work for, began requesting transfers. More important, Jane's group became known as one of the best training grounds and Jane as one of the best teachers and mentors of new talent. Nowhere else did people get the experience, responsibility, and confidence that she cultivated in her employees.

For Chris Morgan, opportunity was short-term and serendipitous. For Jane Adams, opportunity was more long-term, something to be mined methodically. In both cases, though, remaining alert to such variable-term opportunities and being ready to capitalize on them were essential.

Strategic Alliance Building

So far, we have seen how tempered radicals, more or less working alone, can effect change. What happens when these individuals work with allies? Clearly, they gain a sense of legitimacy, access to resources and contacts, technical and task assistance, emotional support, and advice. But they gain much more—the power to move issues to the forefront more quickly and directly than they might by working alone.

When one enlists the help of like-minded, similarly tempered coworkers, the strategic alliance gains clout. That's what happened when a group of senior women at a large professional services firm worked with a group of men sympathetic to their cause. The firm's executive management asked the four-woman group to find out why it was so hard for the company to keep female consultants on staff. In the course of their investigation, the women discussed the demanding culture of the firm: a 70-hour workweek was the norm, and most consultants spent most of their time on the road, visiting clients. The only people who escaped this demanding schedule were part-time consultants, nearly all of whom happened to be women with families. These part-timers were evaluated according to the same performance criteria—including the expectation of long hours—as full-time workers. Though many of the part-timers were talented contributors, they consistently failed to meet the time criterion and so left the company. To correct the problem, the senior women first gained the ear of several executive men who, they knew, regretted missing time with their own families. The men agreed that this was a problem and that the company could not continue to bleed valuable talent. They signed on to help address the issue and, in a matter of months, the evaluation system was adjusted to make success possible for all workers, regardless of their hours.

Tempered radicals don't allow preconceived notions about "the opposition" to get in their way. Indeed, they understand that those who represent the majority perspective are vitally important to gaining support for their cause. Paul Wielgus quietly started a revolution at his company by effectively persuading the opposition to join him. In 1991, Allied Domecq, the global spirits company whose brands include Courvoisier and Beefeater, hired Paul as a marketing director in its brewing and wholesaling division. Originally founded in 1961 as the result of a merger of three British brewing and pub-owning companies, the company had inherited a bureaucratic culture. Tony Hales, the CEO, recognized the need for dramatic change inside the organization and appreciated Paul's talent and fresh perspective. He therefore allowed Paul to quit his marketing job, report directly to the CEO, and found a nine-person learning and training department that ran programs to help participants shake off stodgy thinking and boost their creativity. Yet despite the department's blessing from on high and a two-year record of success, some managers thought of it as fluff. In fact, when David, a senior executive from the internal audit department, was asked to review cases of unnecessary expense, he called Paul on the carpet.

Paul's strategy was to treat David not as a threat but as an equal, even a friend. Instead of being defensive during the meeting, Paul used the opportunity to sell his program. He explained that the trainers worked first with individuals to help unearth their personal values, then worked with them in teams to develop new sets of group values that they all believed in. Next, the trainers aligned these personal and departmental values with those of the company as a whole. "You wouldn't believe the changes, David," he said, enthusiastically. "People come out of these workshops feeling so much more excited about their work. They find more meaning and purpose in it, and as a consequence are happier and much more productive. They call in sick less often, they come to work earlier in the morning, and the ideas they produce are much stronger." Once David understood the value of Paul's program, the two began to talk about holding the training program in the internal audit department itself.

Paul's refusal to be frightened by the system, his belief in the importance of his work, his search for creative and collaborative solutions, his lack of defensiveness with an adversary, and his ability to connect with the auditor paved the way for further change at Allied Domecq. Eventually, the working relationship the two men had formed allowed the internal audit department to transform its image as a policing unit into something more positive. The new Audit Services department came to be known as a partner, rather than an enforcer, in the organization as a whole. And as head of the newly renamed department, David became a strong supporter of Paul's work.

Tempered radicals understand that people who represent the majority perspective can be important allies in more subtle ways as well. In navigating the course between their desire to undo the status quo and the organizational requirements to uphold it, tempered radicals benefit from the advice of insiders who know just how hard to push. When a feminist who wants to change the way her company treats women befriends a conservative Republican man, she knows he can warn her of political minefields. When a Latino manager wants his company to put a Spanish-language version of a manual up on the company's intranet, he knows that the white, monolingual executive who runs operations may turn out to be an excellent advocate.

Of course, tempered radicals know that not everyone is an ally, but they also know it's pointless to see those who represent the status quo as enemies. The senior women found fault with an inequitable evaluation system, not with their male colleagues. Paul won David's help by giving him the benefit of the doubt from the very beginning of their relationship. Indeed, tempered radicals constantly consider all possible courses of action: "Under what conditions, for what issues, and in what circumstances does it make sense to join forces with others?"; "How can I best use this alliance to support my efforts?"

Clearly, there is no one right way to effect change. What works for one individual under one set of circumstances may not work for others under different conditions. The examples above illustrate how tempered radicals use a spectrum of quiet approaches to change their organizations. Some actions are small, private, and muted; some are larger and more public. Their influence spreads as they recruit others and spawn conversations. Top managers can learn a lot from these people about the mechanics of evolutionary change.

Tempered radicals bear no banners; they sound no trumpets. Their ends are sweeping, but their means are mundane. They are firm in their commitments, yet flexible in the ways they fulfill them. Their actions may be small but can spread like a virus. They yearn for rapid change but trust in patience. They often work individually yet pull people together. Instead of stridently pressing their agendas, they start conversations. Rather than battling powerful foes, they seek powerful friends. And in the face of setbacks, they keep going. To do all this, tempered radicals understand revolutionary change for what it is—a phenomenon that can occur suddenly but more often than not requires time, commitment, and the patience to endure.

Originally published in October 2001. Reprint 7923

Notes

1. With the exception of those in the VA hospital and Allied Domecq cases, all the names used through this article are fictitious.

About the Contributors

SIGAL BARSADE is the Joseph Frank Bernstein Professor of Management at Wharton.

RAM CHARAN has been an adviser to the CEOs of some of the world's biggest corporations and their boards. He is a coauthor of *Talent Wins: The New Playbook for Putting People First* (Harvard Business Review Press, 2018).

J. YO-JUD CHENG is an assistant professor of business administration at the University of Virginia's Darden School of Business.

EMILY GANDHI is a senior manager at Wayfair.

ROB GOFFEE is an emeritus professor of organizational behavior at the London Business School.

ADAM GRANT is a professor of management and psychology at the University of Pennsylvania's Wharton School and the author of *Originals: How Non-Conformists Move the World* (Viking, 2016).

BORIS GROYSBERG is the Richard P. Chapman Professor of Business Administration at Harvard Business School and a coauthor, with Michael Slind, of *Talk, Inc.* (Harvard Business Review Press, 2012). Twitter: @bgroysberg.

GARETH JONES is a visiting professor at the IE Business School in Madrid.

JON R. KATZENBACH is a leading practitioner in organizational strategies for Strategy&, PwC's strategy consulting group.

CAROLINE KRONLEY is the president of the Tinker Foundation.

JEREMIAH LEE leads innovation for advisory services at Spencer Stuart. He is a cofounder of two culture-related businesses.

JAY W. LORSCH is the Louis E. Kirstein Professor of Human Relations at Harvard Business School.

ERIN MEYER is a professor at INSEAD and directs two of its executive education programs: Managing Global Virtual Teams and Management Skills for International Business. She is the author of *The Culture Map: Breaking Through the Invisible Boundaries of Global Business* (PublicAffairs, 2014). Twitter: @ErinMeyerINSEAD.

DEBRA E. MEYERSON is a consulting professor of organizational behavior at the Stanford University Graduate School of Education and a faculty research fellow at Stanford's Clayman Institute for Gender Research.

OLIVIA A. O'NEILL is an associate professor of management at George Mason University and a senior scientist at the school's Center for the Advancement of Well-Being.

JESSE PRICE is a leader in organizational culture services at Spencer Stuart. He is a cofounder of two culture-related businesses.

ROBERT E. QUINN is a professor emeritus at the University of Michigan's Ross School of Business and a cofounder of the school's Center for Positive Organizations.

ILONA STEFFEN is a director in the Zurich office of Strategy&.

ANJAN V. THAKOR is the John E. Simon Professor of Finance and the director of doctoral programs at the Olin Business School at Washington University in St. Louis.

PAUL J. ZAK is the founding director of the Center for Neuroeconomics Studies and a professor of economics, psychology, and management at Claremont Graduate University. He is the author of *Trust Factor: The Science of Creating High-Performance Companies* (AMACOM, 2017).

Index

accountability, 55, 135, 155
actions
  daily, meaning from, 87–89
  turning dialogue into, 154–161
Adams, Jane, 169, 178–179
adrenocorticotropin, 54. *See also* stress
Aetna, 93–96, 98, 100–103
affective values, 34. *See also* emotional culture
Allied Domecq, 180–181
ambiguity, 125, 130. *See also* communication
Anderson, Richard, 136, 139–141
anger, 36, 42. *See also* emotional culture
anxiety, 42. *See also* emotional culture
Apple, 84, 96, 118
appraisal systems, 78, 98, 161–162
Arthur Andersen, 99
articulation, of culture, 18. *See also* communication
Arup, 78, 84, 88, 89, 91
aspirational culture, 18–20
attraction-selection-attrition model, 4
attributes, 4–5
authenticity, 67–68, 75–76
authority, 3, 6, 8, 9, 11, 14, 15, 17, 23, 25–30, 89–90. *See also* styles; integrated culture framework
autonomy, 5, 14, 20, 21, 54–55, 90, 139

bad news, 82. *See also* communication
Baker, Doug, 136–139
Bank of America, 69–70
Barry-Wehmiller Companies, 53
Barsafe, Sigal, 33–48
behavioral change, 97–100, 103

beliefs, 104. *See also* change, cultural
biases, 78, 114, 120, 172, 176, 177
Blackberry, 117
BMW, 86, 88
body language, 36, 124
brainstorming, 111. *See also* originality, culture of
Bridgewater, 113, 119
Brown, Dick, 155–158, 161–162
BusinessObjects, 131–132
business performance. *See* performance

candor, 154. *See also* communication
caring, 6–10, 12–17, 20, 23, 25, 26–30, 32, 36. *See also* styles; integrated culture framework
Censeo, 40
challenge stress, 54. *See also* stress
change
  behavior, 97–100, 103
  cultural, 17–21, 69–74, 93–105, 135, 169–172
  incremental, 170–172
  interventions for, 101–103
  response to, 5–7
  by tempered radicals, 165–183
change agents, 73–74, 165–183
Charan, Ram, 147–163
Cheng, J. Yo-Jud, 1–32
Cisco Finance, 38–39
closure, 154. *See also* indecision
cognitive culture, 33–34
cohesion, 45, 109, 116–121
communication
  breakdowns in, 124–125
  dialogue, 148–161
  honesty in, 79–83
  implicit, 124–125, 130
  miscommunication, 123–125

Invaluable insights
always at your fingertips

With an All-Access subscription to
Harvard Business Review, you'll get
so much more than a magazine.

Exclusive online content and tools
you can put to use today

My Library, your personal workspace for sharing,
saving, and organizing HBR.org articles and tools

Unlimited access to more than 4,000 articles in the
Harvard Business Review archive

Subscribe today at hbr.org/subnow

The most important management ideas all in one place.

We hope you enjoyed this book from *Harvard Business Review*. Now you can get even more with HBR's 10 Must Reads Boxed Set. From books on leadership and strategy to managing yourself and others, this 6-book collection delivers articles on the most essential business topics to help you succeed.

HBR's 10 Must Reads Series

The definitive collection of ideas and best practices on our most sought-after topics from the best minds in business.

- Change Management
- Collaboration
- Communication
- Emotional Intelligence
- Innovation
- Leadership
- Making Smart Decisions

- Managing Across Cultures
- Managing People
- Managing Yourself
- Strategic Marketing
- Strategy
- Teams
- The Essentials

hbr.org/mustreads

Buy for your team, clients, or event.
Visit hbr.org/bulksales for quantity discount rates.

Harvard Business Review Press